CHATHAM HOUSE

KOREA AND THE WEST

CHATHAM HOUSE PAPERS · 33

KOREA AND THE WEST

Brian Bridges

The Royal Institute of International Affairs

Routledge & Kegan Paul
London, New York and Andover

First published 1986
by Routledge & Kegan Paul Ltd
11 New Fetter Lane, London EC4P 4EE
29 West 35th Street, New York, NY 10001, USA, and
North Way, Andover, Hants SP10 5BE

Reproduced from copy supplied by
Stephen Austin and Sons Ltd and
printed in Great Britain by
Billing and Son Ltd, Worcester

Library of Congress Cataloging-in-Publication Data

Bridges, Brian, 1948-
Korea and the West.

(Chatham House papers ; 33)
1. Korea (South) – Politics and government.
2. Korea (South) – Foreign relations.
3. Korea (North) – Politics and government.
4. Korea (North) – Foreign relations.
5. Korea (South) – Economic conditions.
6. Korea (North) – Economic conditions.
I. Title.   II. Series: Chatham House papers ; no. 33.
DS917.8.B75   1986   327.519   86-26044

ISBN 0-7102-1110-4

CONTENTS

Contents

ABBREVIATIONS

ANSP	Agency for National Security Planning
ASEAN	Association of South-East Asian Nations
CPC	Central People's Committee
CPD	Council for the Promotion of Democracy
DCRK	Democratic Confederal Republic of Koryo
DJP	Democratic Justice Party
DKP	Democratic Korea Party
DMZ	Demilitarized Zone
EC	European Community
EPB	Economic Planning Board
FAO	Food and Agriculture Organization
GATT	General Agreement on Tariffs and Trade
GNP	Gross National Product
GSP	Generalized System of Preferences
IMF	International Monetary Fund
IOC	International Olympic Committee
KCIA	Korean Central Intelligence Agency
KMA	Korean Military Academy
KNP	Korea National Party
KWP	Korean Workers Party
MFA	Multi-Fibre Agreement
NAM	Non-Aligned Movement
NIC	Newly Industrializing Country
NKDP	New Korea Democratic Party

Abbreviations

OECD	Organization for Economic Cooperation and Development
RPR	Revolutionary Party for Reunification
SITC	Standard International Trade Classification
VTR	Video Tape-Recorder

ACKNOWLEDGMENTS

I would like to thank the many people, in both Europe and Asia, who have given generously of their time and expertise in helping me to understand Korea better. The comments made on the first draft of this paper by the members of a study group held at Chatham House in June 1986 have proved especially useful. In addition, I would like to thank Nigel Pearce for his helpful editing and Patricia Louison for her patient work on the word processor. Finally, I must express my debt of inspiration to Masa Shibusawa, who first encouraged me to 'look east' to Korea.

August 1986   **B.B.**

1

INTRODUCTION

In Tokyo in May 1986, for the second successive year, the leaders of the seven industrialized countries attending the annual economic summit discussed the situation on the Korean peninsula. This reflected not simply the particular sensitivities of the host countries for 1985 and 1986: the Germans' consciousness that, like the Koreans, they were a divided nation, and the Japanese concern to devote some discussion time to Asian questions. It was also evidence of a growing awareness among the seven countries that it was not only Japan and the United States that ought to be interested in Korea. In the month prior to the Tokyo summit, President Chun Doo-hwan became the first ever South Korean president to visit Western Europe, and Mrs Margaret Thatcher became the first British prime minister to visit South Korea. Immediately after the summit, Canadian prime minister Brian Mulroney also visited South Korea.

South Korea's rapid economic growth during the 1970s, despite the rise in energy prices, and its continuing relatively high growth rates after a hiccup in 1980, have made it a leader in that group of states loosely known as the Newly Industrializing Countries (NICs). By 1984, South Korea had a gross national product (GNP) on a par with Austria, a per capita GNP not far below that of Portugal, and a trade volume that made it the fifteenth largest trader in the world, ahead of Australia, India and China. It has continued to maintain its economic dynamism even while, in the last year or two, some of its East Asian rivals have faltered. Yet it is situated in an unpredictable area of tension. Neither the South nor its northern neighbour have

1

been able to trust, or coexist amicably with, each other during the three decades since the fratricidal Korean War. Two events in 1983 – the destruction of the KAL airliner by a Soviet fighter and the bomb attack in Rangoon, in which four South Korean cabinet ministers were killed by North Korean agents – highlight the tension which still surrounds the Korean peninsula.

The aim of this paper is to analyse the political and economic situation in the two Koreas, both internal and external, as well as to examine the extent of West European involvement and interests in developments on the peninsula. The intricate politics of a divided country are reflected in the rhetoric of self-justificatory claims by both Koreas, but the dearth of systematic data and reliable information on the closed society of North Korea inevitably places the emphasis of the study on the South. Nevertheless, wherever possible, North Korean policies and perceptions will be considered. (For the sake of simplicity, I have used the terms North and South Korea throughout, rather than their official names, which are respectively the People's Democratic Republic of Korea and the Republic of Korea.)

Despite a common linguistic, historical and cultural background, the political systems of the two states which have existed north and south of the 38th parallel since 1948 today share little except a concentration of power in the hands of a few. The leaders of both countries have tried to establish the legitimacy of their own rule, and, by extension, their right to the whole peninsula. In the North a totalitarian system is trying to arrange a dynastic succession, while, in the South, an authoritarian system is moving gingerly towards constitutional democracy. Chapter 2 examines the political structure of the two countries and the nature of the internal tensions produced, more visibly in the South, by the need to marry political development with socio-economic modernization.

Despite the lack of reliable North Korean data, it is clear that over the last three decades both North and South have succeeded in turning war-shattered economies into sizeable industrial complexes with good rates of growth. Nevertheless, over the last decade or so, it is the South Korean economy which has made the most impressive advances, so that its GNP is now probably around three times that of the North. This divergence has had an effect on the relatively closed economy of the North, which is now considering changes in its economic orientation in order to try to compete. Chapter 3 examines the characteristic economic development and the potentialities for growth in both countries.

The dynamic of inter-Korean rivalry is one of the driving forces behind the South's – and no doubt also the North's – attempts to excel. This competition has been apparent not only politically and economically, but also, as Chapter 4 shows, in the military and diplomatic spheres. Even though the precarious truce on the border has survived for more than 30 years, the legacy of the Korean War remains a powerful one; the two Koreas, unlike the two Germanies, have kept themselves and their people well apart. Chapter 4, therefore, also examines the nature of and motivations behind the current intermittent dialogue between the two Koreas.

A Korean proverb warns that the prawn (Korea) will have its back broken by the convulsions of the whales (neighbouring great powers). Chapter 5 considers the economic and politico-strategic interests of the four interested major powers – China, the Soviet Union, Japan and the United States. Despite certain common denominators, the four powers see their bilateral interests in the two Korean states from differing perspectives; this in turn gives both North and South Korea some room for diplomatic manoeuvring.

For West Europeans there is a lack of depth, and even an element of novelty, in their relationship with the two Koreas. They have had relatively few economic and political interests in either Korea until recently, even though several West European countries sent troops to fight in the Korean War. Chapter 6 examines the gradual changes in the interests of Western Europe – primarily the European Community (EC) and its constituent members – in the developments on, and surrounding, the Korean peninsula. The conclusion suggests a number of ways in which European governments as well as the private sector might utilize the opportunities available if the Euro-Korean relationship is to avoid the somewhat sterile route that Euro-Japanese relations took in the late 1970s.

If, as some people would argue, the centre of global power is shifting, at least economically, from the Atlantic to the Pacific, South Korea (and North Korea too, if it becomes less isolationist) will become an increasingly important actor on the international stage. In September 1988 its capital city, Seoul, will be the host to the Olympic Games; the spring of that year should see the first ever peaceful transfer of power in the South; in 1988, too, South Korea hopes to become a member of the Organization for Economic Cooperation and Development (OECD). That kind of political and economic maturity, if achieved, will make it impossible for the West to ignore the Korean peninsula.

2
POLITICAL CULTURE IN THE TWO KOREAS

The two halves of Korea have many things in common – their ancestry, language, historical legacy, and underlying cultural heritage. However, the strength of traditional beliefs and values has been tempered by the divergent and ideologically polarized systems that have been developed over the past four decades north and south of the border.

Geography has clearly played an important role in the development of the Korean people and their character. The peninsula itself, about 620 miles (992 km) long and 120 miles (192 km) wide at its narrowest point, is roughly the area of the United Kingdom; it is a highly mountainous area and has a coastline dotted with numerous small islands. Apart from a few mineral resources in the northern part, it has no valuable natural resources. The toughness of the land – and the extremes of climate – have produced a resilient and, indeed, a very homogeneous people. Korea's geopolitical situation has required its inhabitants to develop both patience and adaptability, but it has not subdued their pride or spirit.[1]

The fact that Korea became a basically unified country under the Silla kingdom in 668 – and remained that way, apart from occasional and brief periods of political division, until 1945 – has given the Koreans a strong sense of political continuity, unequalled except by the Chinese. Medieval Korea was one of the most centralized and uniformly administered states in pre-colonial Asia, but it never had a fully autocratic system, in the way that the Japanese emperor became divinized or the Chinese emperor was potentially absolute. Despite the strength of Chinese cultural influences, which were at

5

their most evident under the Yi dynasty (1392–1910), when Korea became almost a Confucian model of intellectual life and political institution, some of the traditional social structures survived. Power was exercised through the *yangban* (aristocracy), which nevertheless suffered from rivalry between competing cliques of nobles and officials. Factionalism, which has never really been eliminated from Korean politics, gradually became a predominant characteristic. By the eighteenth and nineteenth centuries, therefore, Korea was suffering from a lack of strong central leadership and from political stagnation. It had become so weak, politically and economically, that it could offer humiliatingly little resistance to annexation by the Japanese in 1910. The Japanese occupation until 1945 gained only minimal acceptance from the Koreans, but, apart from intermittent and ineffective guerrilla warfare and the nationwide demonstration for independence on 1 March 1919, Japanese control was as total as it was brutal. The Japanese tried to crush the Korean national identity; unwillingly, and at times unconsciously, the Koreans fell under the sway of Japanese patterns and habits that were largely alien to their traditional culture. The legacy of bitterness between the Koreans and Japanese left by the manner of this occupation is still relevant today.

The Koreans saw the Allied victory over Japan as the chance to regain their lost independence, even though they would not have the satisfaction of winning it with their own hands. However, the Yalta and Potsdam Conferences in 1945 had agreed in principle that there should be Soviet and US occupation zones in Korea for the initial purposes of disarming and evacuating the Japanese. In mid-August 1945, the US army drew a zonal boundary along the 38th parallel, which lies some 30 miles north of Seoul and was about as northerly a line as the Soviets could be expected to accept. This division led to the emergence of two separate entities north and south of that line, which has effectively remained the border ever since. After elections in the southern part, sponsored by the United Nations, the United States terminated its occupation in August 1948 in favour of the new government of the Republic of Korea, headed by President Syngman Rhee. A few weeks later, in September 1948, in the northern part, the Democratic People's Republic of Korea was established under Soviet auspices, with Kim Il-sung as prime minister. Sporadic violence occurred along the border, and in June 1950 the North tried to abolish this artificial division by force. The poorly organized

South Korean troops were driven back to the very southern tip of the peninsula, but were saved by the intervention of the United Nations (UN). Following the dramatic Inchon landing in September 1950, the North Korean forces were pushed back across the 38th parallel and even as far as the Yalu river, which marks the boundary between Korea and China. This in turn prompted intervention by Chinese 'volunteers', and the UN forces were pushed back south again. By the spring of 1951, however, the front line was stabilized virtually where it had been before the fighting started, although it was not until July 1953 that an armistice was signed.

The manner of the creation of the two governments in 1948, and the character of the leaders that survived the harrowing events of 1950–3, made a crucial imprint on the political evolution of the two Koreas. Both have highly centralized political systems with an overwhelming concentration of power in the hands of the top leader. In the North, a family-style communist system is trying to arrange a dynastic succession, while, in the South, an authoritarian system now dominated by the military is gradually moving towards constitutional democracy. Although the systems have diverged in form, in substance North and South share one dominant ideology: nationalism. The humiliating experiences of Japanese colonization and the traumas of the Korean War and its foreign interventions have only fuelled traditional Korean pride. The search for political, economic, and military independence by the two Koreas can therefore be seen as an expression of Korean nationalism.

The presidential system in South Korea

President Chun has made one of the major themes of his speeches over the last few years a promise to step down after the expiry of the seven-year term allowed under the present constitution and so become the first South Korean leader to achieve a peaceful transition of power.

The first president, the veteran fighter for independence, Syngman Rhee, took strong and often suspect measures to ensure his survival in power. Electoral corruption reached a peak in the 1960 elections and led to massive demonstrations, spearheaded by students. Rhee was forced to resign, and a cabinet system, headed by Chang Myon, replaced the presidential system. However, as opinion within the country became increasingly polarized, the military staged a coup in

May 1961. Major-General Park Chung-hee emerged as the strong man of the new government. He retired from the army, was elected as president in 1963 and twice again for four-year terms, until, in 1972, he introduced the Yushin (Revitalizing) Constitution, which gave him sweeping powers and effectively made him president for life. Although the country made significant economic progress during his years in power, he was not prepared to allow any comparable progress in the political sphere. Student opposition again began to grow in the late 1970s, and the differences which emerged within the leadership about how to deal with this prompted Kim Jae-kyu, the head of the Korean Central Intelligence Agency (KCIA), to assassinate Park in October 1979.

An academic turned politician, Choi Kyu-hah, became acting president and was elected president in December 1979, but the state of martial law gave the military, and one group in particular, headed by Major-General Chun, greater power. The military became increasingly worried by student and labour unrest and by the links between these groups and opposition politicians such as Kim Dae-jung, who had strongly challenged Park in the 1971 parliamentary election. In May 1980, Kim was arrested and a week-long revolt by students and others in Kwangju was bloodily suppressed by the army. Effective power was ebbing away from Choi; in August Chun resigned from the army and succeeded him as president. A referendum in October 1980 approved a new constitution, under which the president is elected by an electoral college of more than 5,000 members (who are in turn elected by direct and universal vote) for one seven-year term, with no extension. In February 1981, Chun was re-elected president.

Chun was born in 1931 in the south-eastern province of Kyong-sang, which has traditionally provided Korean leaders, and graduated from the Korean Military Academy (KMA) in 1955 as a member of the eleventh class, the first class to receive US-oriented training. Chun is thus a more 'American product' of the Korean military establishment than his predecessor Park, who had trained and served under the Japanese army. He also served as a regimental commander in Vietnam, and, in 1979, he held an important post in the Defence Security Command, which has responsibility for military counter-intelligence. Having taken power by what was in reality a military coup, Chun has been sensitive to domestic criticism of the legitimacy of his rule.

Although Chun was critical of his predecessor Park for holding the reins of power too long and cloaking his repressive measures with the mantle of national security, he himself shares with Park the tendency to stress the commitment to national security above all else. There is also continuity in another sense: a belief that Western-style democracy is not suitable for Korean soil and that it needs to be adapted to Korea's peculiar history, culture and values. The predilection for ideological simplicity and rigidity in contemporary South Korean politics derives from the anti-communist commitment, but it is also, in part, a continuation of the Confucian tradition of ideological orthodoxy (a tendency not weakened by the ideological indoctrination imposed on the Koreans towards the end of the Japanese period of rule). Anti-communism has become an important political symbol in postwar South Korea; for Chun, the line separating democratic socialism from revolutionary communism is an extremely thin one. Actual or perceived threats from North Korea thus serve as a justification for the strong methods of government and the limited toleration of opposition. This has led, as Amnesty International and other organizations have documented, to the harassment, imprisonment and even torture of anti-government demonstrators and critics.

In a manner that echoed Park's actions after his coup in 1961, Chun proclaimed a 'new era' when he came to power. He dissolved all the former political parties, banned over 500 politicians and party members from political activity for eight years, and purged several thousand bureaucrats associated with the previous regime. He installed his new, less ideological generation in power. Some of his military colleagues were moved into office, with those from the same, eleventh, class of the KMA getting key army and security posts. He reorganized the KCIA, renaming it the Agency for National Security Planning (ANSP), as well as the presidential secretariat at the Blue House, so as to make the president more accessible to cabinet members.

Nevertheless, it remains questionable how important cabinet ministers are in the decision-making process. There have been a succession of cabinet reshuffles since Chun became president; several in the early years of his rule were necessitated by financial scandals in which even members of his own family were implicated. Lho Shin-yong, appointed as prime minister in February 1985, is the fifth prime minister in as many years. It is widely thought, therefore, that, rather than rely on the cabinet, the president takes on the tasks of overall decision-making with the help of a small group of advisers, which includes both economic technocrats and retired military officers. The military is still the most powerful group in the country, even though Chun is clearly in control. Yet his authority derives as much from the Confucian traditions of obedience as it does from military authoritarianism, and it has been enhanced by some successes he has gained in restoring the economy after the disastrous year of 1980, when negative growth was recorded, and in securing greater prestige for South Korea on the international stage. However, the lack of depth of popular support was made only too clear by the February 1985 National Assembly elections.

Parliamentary and extra-parliamentary opposition
These were the second parliamentary elections to be held since Chun came to power, and it had been widely expected that, as in the March 1981 elections, Chun's own party, the Democratic Justice Party (DJP), would win easily. Not only were significantly greater resources at the DJP's disposal, but the election rules favour the largest party. Two-thirds of the seats go to representatives elected from 92 two-member constituencies, but the remaining third of these seats are filled on a proportional representation system, under which 61 seats are awarded to the party with the highest number of constituency-member seats and the rest (31) are divided proportionally among the other parties. However, the emergence of a new opposition party, the New Korea Democratic Party (NKDP), less than a month before the election date altered the complexion of the campaign.

In the 1981 elections, the DJP had easily outshone the newly created opposition parties, the Korea National Party (KNP) and Democratic Korea Party (DKP), which had relatively unknown leaders. Kim Dae-jung had been in prison then, although his death sentence in September 1980 on charges of attempted rebellion had been commuted, after considerable pressure from the US and other foreign governments, to life imprisonment in January 1981. The following year Chun reduced the sentence to 20 years' imprisonment, and in mid-December 1982 he allowed Kim to leave for medical treatment in the United States. Kim's return from exile, six days before the 1985 elections, greatly encouraged the opposition.

Between March 1983 and November 1984 Chun had removed successive groups of former politicians from the banned list, with the exception of fourteen people, a group which included the political heavyweights, the 'three Kims': Kim Dae-jung; Kim Jong-pil, a former prime minister, who was also away in the United States (from July 1984 until February 1986); and Kim Young-sam, leader of the defunct New Democratic Party, who in May 1983 had actually undertaken a 23-day hunger strike for political democracy. Chun also made a number of other moves in the months leading up to February 1985 which, while not representing the democratic liberalization that the various opposition groups were demanding, did suggest cautious steps in that direction. Riot police were withdrawn from university campuses, and students were allowed to demonstrate, provided that their demonstrations were confined to the campuses alone. Stringent press controls were relaxed slightly to permit a limited amount of reporting of strikes, demonstrations and opposition criticisms of the government. The establishment of an independent opposition party, the NKDP, was tolerated, and Kim Dae-jung was allowed to return from exile.

The NKDP consists of two broad groups, those affiliated to the Council for the Promotion of Democracy (CPD) and those not, with the former group in turn subdivided into factions supporting Kim Young-sam and Kim Dae-jung (although neither could formally become party members, since their political rights were restricted). The NKDP therefore contains many of the factional characteristics of Korean political life, and the government evidently expected these internal differences to weaken the new party. South Korean political groups tend to be dominated by leaders whose authority depends on personal appeal rather than on organizational strength; accordingly, mere clashes of personality can spur intra- or inter-party conflicts.

The NKDP, conscious of the need to differentiate itself from the other opposition parties, not only publicly challenged Chun's legitimacy but also openly discussed questions, such as the handling of the 1980 Kwangju uprising and Chun's wife's ties to various financial scandals, which had previously been considered taboo. The government, pledged to conduct a 'fair and honest election' (not least because Chun was anxious to project an image of moderation in order to secure a prestige-boosting invitation to the United States in the spring), tolerated this measure of freedom of speech.

The DJP retained its predominant position by polling strongly in the country areas and gaining 35 per cent of the overall vote, only one percentage point down on the 1981 figure. The surprising vote came for the NKDP, which managed to outperform both the more established opposition parties. By drawing strong support from Seoul and other cities, it took as much as 29 per cent of the total vote. Nevertheless, the proportional representation system widened the gap to give the DJP 148 seats to the NKDP's 67. However, the poor performance of the DKP, which gained only 35 seats, led to its break-up and, in early April, the majority of the DKP assemblymen defected to the NKDP. Thus, although the KNP does still exist as a small party of 20 assemblymen, the NKDP's strength has helped to transform the National Assembly into a *de facto* two-party system.

The extent of popular support for the NKDP surprised the government. Chun appeared to accept the need for further compromise, and lifted the ban on the remaining fourteen politicians, though making it clear that Kim Dae-jung, still under suspended sentence, could not join a political party. Chun also reshuffled his cabinet and appointed another retired general from the eleventh class, Roh Tae-woo, as the new chairman of the DJP, in order to try to restore its battered prestige. Roh has since not only reorganized the DJP but consolidated his position as its most likely contender to succeed Chun.

When in the second half of 1985 the NKDP began to campaign for Chun to revise the constitution so as to remove the electoral college system, which was felt to be subject to government manipulation, and called on him to step down before the end of his term, the limits to his toleration were revealed. He rejected the NKDP's demands, harassed the two Kims, started to crack down on the students after a group of them had occupied the US Information Service library in May and then attempted occupations of the DJP offices and other buildings later in the year, and warned that the planned NKDP/CPD campaign to obtain 10 million signatures to a petition demanding constitutional revision was illegal.

More subtly, the government tried to play upon the factionalism within the NKDP by talking with the party's president, Lee Min-woo, rather than with the two Kims, and by not discouraging Kim Young-sam from actually becoming a party member, thereby distancing him slightly from Kim Dae-jung, who has to remain outside the formal party structure because his civil rights remain suspended.

This tactic yielded some reward, in that a small group of a dozen assemblymen, disillusioned by personal and policy differences between the two Kims, split away to form the New Conservative Group. Furthermore, the tougher line that the government began to take towards opposition activities suggested that the pendulum which, since the events of 1960, has swung between the two strands of Korean political consciousness – the desire for freedom and the demand for order – was again swinging away from the former to the latter.

The political role of the military, or the retired military, has always been distrusted by the South Korean people. Various discontented segments of the population have found a – possibly temporary – common cause in opposing Chun and his new political structure and in supporting the NKDP both before and after the 1985 elections. A number of journalists and academics were removed when Chun came to power, and, although the press is no longer subject to the formal restrictions typical of the Park era, the required practice of 'self-censorship' does impose a limitation on the freedom of expression for writers. Government control over broadcasting has remained even more direct, and in February 1986 a campaign was launched to protest against the bias of the state-owned Korea Broadcasting System (KBS) television network with a refusal to pay for subscription fees.

The students have been restless; both they and the Chun government are aware of the precedent of decisive student influence during the events of 1960. The students have grievances about facilities and courses, as well as about close police supervision, but they are also showing signs of increasing radicalization. One government response to that tendency, a proposal in mid-1985 to introduce a campus stabilization law, under which a non-judicial panel would have sent militant students off for a six-month 'reorientation programme', had to be dropped because of the controversy it provoked. Student demonstrations during 1986, although on a smaller scale than demonstrations of earlier years, have been characterized by a greater militancy and a rising tone of anti-Americanism. Less appreciative of the US role in defending the country than their elders, who experienced the Korean War, the students have given a deeper resonance to the latent anti-Americanism (social rather than strictly political) already existing in Korean society. However, when a number of opposition party rallies (notably the 3 May meeting in

13

Inchon) were broken up by violent student radicals, there was a backlash among middle-class Koreans. Even among the students opinion has been divided, with some urging tactical restraint and others arguing for radical action (a few students have even burnt themselves to death).

The students' demands for rapid democratization have received some public support from university professors. Sympathetic chords have been struck with organized, and unorganized, labour, which also shows signs of becoming more radicalized. However, the government – through strict labour legislation introduced in 1980 – and big business – by often refusing to accept company unions – are determined to keep the unions weak. Although, as will be shown in the next chapter, income distribution is relatively equitable by developing-country standards, the rapid pace of socio-economic modernization has left some industrial workers and farmers suffering from economic injustice and its consequent social ills. Chun and, by extension, the United States have been blamed by these discontented elements of the labour movement.

The Christian churches, which claim over twenty per cent of the population as believers, have also been critical of human rights abuses, but, until recently, have been less vocal under Chun than under Park. Again, a split seems to be occurring between the more activist, such as Revd Moon Ik-hwan, chairman of the *Mintongnyon* (an umbrella organization of Christian groups formed in 1985), who was arrested in May 1986 for inciting students to riot, and the less activist but nonetheless concerned church leaders, such as the Catholic primate Cardinal Stephen Kim, who has called for rapid constitutional revision but stressed the need for a peaceful transition to democracy.

In early 1986, therefore, Chun and the opposition seemed set on a collision course as Kim Young-sam and some NKDP assemblymen were either put under house arrest temporarily or questioned by the police, and the signature-gathering campaign was launched in mid-February. Around 700,000 signatures were collected for the petition in the first month. At the same time, events in the Philippines served to worry the government and inspire the opposition groups. As a result, Chun, while making it clear that 'people power' on the Filipino model would not be applicable to South Korea, did decide to meet the opposition party leaders. He carefully made a number of concessions to the opposition political parties, culminating in the establishment at the end of June of a special committee in the National Assembly to draft constitutional amendments. The government has also begun to release some political prisoners.

Chun's moves have done much to dilute criticisms from the KNP, which has been reluctant to support the extra-parliamentary signature campaign, and have caused arguments within the NKDP over the appropriate response. Certainly, the increasing radicalization of the students and some other opposition groups has worried not only the government but also the NKDP, which fears that it might be losing the middle ground in a more polarized political climate. Some NKDP leaders have been publicly critical of the students' violence and anti-US rhetoric, and during the period of the sixth anniversary of the Kwangju uprising the NKDP interrupted a series of nation-wide rallies to avoid confrontation with the government forces. In addition, the evident reluctance of the United States to be drawn into open criticism of the Chun administration reinforced the feeling of some NKDP leaders, particularly Kim Youngsam's faction, that compromise was necessary. The government has already passed a law, though delayed its implementation, granting local political autonomy; if a compromise on further constitutional change is reached by the end of 1986, it is possible that local, National Assembly and presidential elections could all be held during 1987.

There is, of course, a difference between agreeing to discuss constitutional revision and actually accepting changes that would satisfy the opposition. Certainly, with the DJP apparently now favouring a cabinet-style parliamentary system and the KNP and the NKDP a presidential system by direct election, a gap remains. Compromise is not always a noted characteristic of Korean politics, but, in private, politicians from both the government and the opposition parties feel that one can, and must, be reached.

Although Chun's government and the parliamentary opposition disagree on the fundamental question of the restoration of democracy, on a number of other issues there is little between them. There is almost complete agreement on a dislike for communism, a pro-US foreign policy, military vigilance against North Korea, and the broad continuation of the present economic system. However disenchanted the South Korean opposition groups may be with Chun's authoritarian rule, a combination of anti-communist indoctrination, strict anti-communist legislation, and lingering and still vivid memories of North Korean atrocities in the South during the Korean War keeps them solidly behind the government in opposing North Korean-style communism.

The North Korean political system
The last 40 years have seen several transfers of power in South Korea, and it is again facing the trauma of succession. For North Korea, there has been no such transfer of power – the death of Enver Hoxha of Albania in 1985 made Kim Il-sung the longest-serving ruler in the world – but it too is now facing the crucial problem of succession.

As a communist state, North Korea has an official ideology that guides its political life and a ruling party that applies this ideology to practical policies. However, the centralized control which demands total loyalty to the leader, and more recently to his son as well, has produced a pervasive and almost suffocating cult of personality that has no current equivalent in any other communist country.

It is difficult to separate fact from fiction in the efforts of the North Korean media to propagate the personality cult surrounding Kim Il-sung and his family. Although Kim may not be a particularly charismatic figure, he has shown himself to be a survivor and a master of political intrigue. He came to power in North Korea with the blessings and help of the Soviet army (after fighting against the Japanese in Manchuria in 1937–41, he fled to the Soviet Maritime Provinces), and in the late 1940s and early 1950s he was able to fight off challenges from other factions within the communist movement, such as local communists and returnees from parts of China and the Soviet Union. Since 1958 he has been unchallenged. He came to exercise effective control through the unified Korean Workers Party (KWP), of which he was chairman, while being concurrently prime minister.

However, after 1972, when a new constitution was promulgated, Kim gradually began to shift his centre of power from the party to the state, although the considerable overlap of personnel in the top echelons of party and government blurs the distinctions between the two. The new constitution declared Kim's political thought, *juche* (self-reliance), to be the ideology of the state; established his revolutionary tradition as the tradition of Korea; and created a new post, the president of the republic (to which Kim was elected in

December 1972), as well as a new powerful administrative organ – a kind of 'super-cabinet' known as the Central People's Committee (CPC). Although the constitution sanctioned the rule of the KWP, in practice the office of president and the CPC have gradually undermined the pre-eminence of the KWP Politburo. The KWP's Central Committee plenums have become more infrequent, as indeed have Party Congresses (the Seventh Party Congress, due in 1984, has yet to take place), while, on the other hand, the annual sessions of the Supreme People's Assembly (the parliament elected every four years), rather than being largely ceremonial, have come to discuss more important issues.[2]

The constitution does not provide a procedure for the succession (there is no stipulation for a vice-president to succeed automatically) and, as Kim enters his mid-seventies and doubts about his health increase, it is the succession which has now become the nub of interest in North Korean politics. Kim, after becoming president, decided to yield operation of the party to his son, Jong-il, who in 1974 took over party organizational, propaganda and agitational responsibilities. From the mid-1970s, the North Korean media began to refer favourably to the 'party centre' (the code word for Kim Jong-il), and at the Sixth KWP Party Congress in 1980 Kim Jong-il's emergence as a political leader was publicized; his name was listed fourth in the KWP Politburo and second in the KWP Secretariat. The North Korean media began to feature him as the 'dear leader' following in the footsteps of his father, the 'great leader', and in July 1984 it was finally announced that the son was the 'sole successor' to the father.

A number of factors seem to lie behind Kim's decision to promote his son as his successor. First, it arose from an attempt to reconcile two not totally compatible goals: namely, to modernize the Korean economy and society, and yet to maintain the revolutionary zeal that he and the early leaders of the KWP possessed. Kim has endeavoured to keep the population ideologically mobilized through such mass organizations as the Socialist Working Youth League (ages 14–28), the Korean Democratic Women's League and the Korean Federation of Trade Unions (each of which has three million members). Yet industrialization has brought a rise in the number of engineers and technicians, many of whom have experience of life abroad, mainly through training in the Soviet Union. As the KWP has tried to expand its numbers – and by the

17

early 1980s two million people or 10 per cent of the population, a percentage much higher than in China or the Soviet Union, were members – many from this technical intelligentsia have been admitted to party membership. Although the party has made every effort to imbue them with the ideology of Kim Il-sung, technocrats are unlikely to have the same outlook and concerns as first-generation revolutionaries. Kim will have watched the fate of the Soviet and Chinese parties after the demise of dominant leaders; both were to a certain extent deradicalized, and the emphasis shifted to less ideological economic development. In North Korea, the ideological revolution has needed to be upheld, and the possibility of revisionist tendencies emerging after Kim's death has to be guarded against.

Second, someone was needed who would not only carry on the socialist revolution in Korea, but who would continue Kim's own personal brand of revolutionary thought, *juche*. In the 1950s Kim described *juche* as the 'creative' application of Marxism-Leninism to the 'concrete conditions' of the North Korean situation; by the 1980s *juche* had come to supercede Marxism-Leninism (Kim's four-hour-long main report to the 1980 Party Congress failed to mention the latter concept once). To Kim, *juche* means 'independence in politics, self-reliance in the economy, and self-defence in national defence'. *Juche* was to provide the key to the transformation from socialism to communism (North Korea was deemed to have reached the stage of socialism in 1958) by means of the implementation of the three revolutionary lines – the ideological, cultural and technical revolutions. The term itself is vague enough to admit a number of connotations, but also appeals to Korean nationalist sentiments; by extension, it obviates the need to acknowledge ideological and material debts to the Soviet and Chinese communist parties. In North Korea, in fact, *juche* has become more than just a political slogan; it is virtually an all-encompassing philosophy. And now the younger Kim is credited with pointing up new tenets of this ideology and its application to everyday life.[3]

Third, there was a need to find someone who would be totally loyal to Kim during his lifetime: in Kim's own words, someone who would be 'boundlessly faithful to the party and revolution'. After toying in the early 1970s with the idea of grooming his younger brother, Yong-ju, Kim decided upon the only surviving son of his first marriage, Jong-il, still only 40 in 1980, thereby effectively missing out a generation in the power structure. The subsequent hagiography devoted to idolizing Jong-il's late mother has reportedly not been well received by Kim Il-sung's present wife, who is seldom mentioned in the media.

Although information is patchy, events such as the purge of several top generals in the 1968–70 period, the disappearance from public view after 1977 of the then third-ranking Kim Tong-gyu, as well as the large turnovers in membership of the KWP Central Committee, suggest that there can be personality and political differences among the North Korean elite. There are signs, too, of a certain amount of passive resistance to the installation of Kim Jong-il as successor to his father. This could come from party ideologues who regard the hereditary transfer of power as ideological anathema as well as from those technocrats who have little real commitment to '*juche* orientation'. In 1982, a number of senior military officers fled to China, reportedly dissatisfied with the succession plans. In mid-1983, Japanese reports suggested that over a thousand party members had been purged since the beginning of that year for opposing the son's succession. Moreover, in January 1985, the KWP adopted a slogan calling for 'a relentless fight against all unhealthy elements', and, even in May 1986, the elder Kim felt the need to warn against factionalism within the KWP and spoke of the 'serious ideological struggle to eliminate the outdated remnants still seen among the functionaries'.[4] In August 1985, the Soviet press reported that hundreds of North Koreans were engaged in effectively forced labour, such as railway construction and lumbering in Siberia; politically unreliable elements are believed to be part of this contingent.

Yet, apart from his father's endorsement, the younger Kim seems to have built up certain power bases of his own. His work within the KWP and the 'Three Revolution Squads' (small groups of young people, including non-party members, sent out to factories and cooperative farms to encourage productivity) has given him some support among the new generations. Certain military leaders, such as Defence Minister Oh Chin-u and Chairman of the Joint Chiefs of Staff Oh Kuk-ryol, who was a classmate of Jong-il's at the Mangyongdae Revolutionary Academy (a special educational institution for leadership training with the emphasis on ideological and military skills) are believed to support him, as does the Prime Minister, Kang Song-san (also a graduate of Mangyongdae). Both Oh Kuk-ryol and Kang are sons of earlier revolutionary comrades of Kim Il-sung. Kim Jong-il may also be benefiting from his efforts to claim credit for the wider access to foreign consumer goods for party cadres and technicians.

While the available evidence suggests that the younger Kim does have enough visible support, and, as such, is likely to succeed on his father's death, views differ as to the policies he will adopt. Some observers argue that, because he lacks his father's revolutionary credentials, the younger Kim will be forced to prove himself by some adventurous act against the South (he is often credited with responsibility for organizing the bomb explosion which killed four senior South Korean cabinet members in Rangoon in 1983). Others disagree, feeling that when the older Kim dies, the North Koreans will be freed from his obsession; the younger Kim's legitimacy will be based more on his ability as an administrator than on whether or not he is a good revolutionary, and the commitments to forceful reunification will become more ritualistic.

Kim Jong-il is reportedly already exercising day-to-day control over the party and chairing Politburo meetings; he has already been named Supreme Commander of the Armed Forces. Like his father before him, he is embarking on a series of visits around the country to carry out self-proclaimed 'on-the-spot guidance'. He has yet to be given any formal state post and is not yet a member of the important CPC, but that is not expected to be long delayed. Nevertheless, the element of uncertainty remains. Even if the elder Kim survives for a while yet, so postponing the actual resolution of the succession question and allowing the younger Kim to consolidate his position further, there are a number of issues, relating particularly to the economy and the need for modern technology and to the North-South dialogue, which are already presenting the North Korean leadership with important decisions on the weight to be given to ideological as against pragmatic considerations.

3

ECONOMIC DEVELOPMENT

When Korea was divided in 1945, most of the industrial raw materials, the heavy industry developed by the Japanese, and the coal and hydroelectric power sources passed to North Korea, whereas the South inherited most of the strategic harbours, the best agricultural land, considerable light industry and well over half the population. In both North and South the rehabilitative efforts to create viable, stable economies out of what had become part-economies after 1945 had to be restarted after the destruction wreaked by the Korean War. Both states have made significant economic progress since, though at differing times and with different results. Both now face economic problems, though these seem less serious for the South than for the North.

The basis of South Korean growth
The World Bank has noted how the South Korea of the early 1960s, then 'one of the poorest developing countries', had been transformed, by the late 1970s, into 'a semi-industrial, middle-income country with a strong external payments position'. By the mid-1980s, it had become a leader in that group of countries loosely known as the NICs. As Table 3.1 shows, per capita GNP (expressed in current prices) rose from only $80 in 1960 to over $2,000 in the mid-1980s; annual per capita growth rates averaged nearly 7 per cent in real terms. ($ in this paper refers to US dollars throughout).

Table 3.1 Growth of South Korean GNP, 1955–85

	1955	1960	1970	1980	1985
GNP ($ bn)	1.4	2.0	7.8	56.5	83.1
Per capita GNP ($)	67	80	243	1,481	2,032
Average GNP growth rate (%)	—	3.7 (1953–60)	8.5 (1961–70)	8.1 (1971–80)	7.5 (1981–5)

Source: Statistics from the South Korean Economic Planning Board and Bank of Korea, Seoul (various years).

A number of contributing factors can be suggested to explain this progress, although observers dispute their relative influence: a firm commitment to development; a strong partnership between government and business; a well-educated, disciplined and industrious workforce; and positive, but to a certain extent selective, integration with the international economy. South Korea has in several respects followed the 'model' of its nearest capitalist neighbour, Japan – probably more than Koreans themselves wish to admit and less than outside observers often suspect.

South Korea does share with Japan, and with the other three Asian NICs (Hong Kong, Singapore and Taiwan) with which it is most often associated, a serious lack of natural resources. But like them it is committed to utilizing to the utmost its human resources, by drawing on what has sometimes been characterized as a Confucian legacy of education, discipline, thrift and diligence. Japan grew through a mix of free-market competition and government guidance. Its postwar domestic industrial buildup fuelled rapid growth rates in exports as it turned towards the international market-place. Lacking the large domestic market that Japan possesses, the four Asian NICs have not followed exactly the same path. Hong Kong has always been outward-oriented, but the other three NICs did not begin to give priority to manufactured export-oriented growth strategies until the 1960s. At the risk of over-simplification, Japan has gradually shifted from heavy industry into lighter, more capital-intensive assembly-type operations, whereas, for the NICs, the emphasis has been on light, labour-intensive industries first followed by a move, in South Korea, Singapore and Taiwan, into certain heavy industries, often with mixed results. Hong Kong has continued to focus on light manufacturing industries. Japan avoided external debt and restrained inward investment, whereas South Korea relied on foreign loans, and Hong Kong, Singapore and Taiwan used foreign investment to varying degrees to finance capital requirements. Some of the characteristics of South Korean development should now be examined.

(a)   The commitment to development planning

Despite the considerable US aid contributions to the recovery of the South Korean economy after the Korean War (economic assistance reached $1.86 billion during 1953–9, as compared with an estimated war damage of $6 bn), not until 1957 did per capita income return to the pre-Korean War level. Even by the early 1960s, South Korea still suffered from a heavy dependency on agriculture and a chronic balance-of-payments deficit. President Rhee had seemed, if anything, more concerned with political manoeuvring than with long-term economic development; but President Park made economic planning a central plank of his policies. Concrete economic performance became the touchstone of political success and national progress. He inaugurated a series of five-year economic development plans, beginning in 1962.

During the First Plan (1962–6), the principal objective was to establish the foundations of a self-reliant economy by securing energy supply sources, expanding key industries, developing the social infrastructure and improving the balance of payments. During the Second Plan (1967–71), the emphasis was laid more on the modernization of the industrial structure; labour-intensive manufacturing was seen as the most rapid source of economic growth and export industries were encouraged at the expense of other sectors. By the late 1960s, the rural/urban gap was growing dangerously, so the Third Plan (1972–6) emphasized more balanced growth in the various regions of the country and the maximization of land cultivation through the *Saemaul* (New Village) Movement, but also concentrated on building up the heavy and chemical industries. South Korea weathered the oil shocks of 1973–4 and the subsequent recession largely by the assiduous diversification of its export markets, and the Fourth Plan (1977–81) tried to work towards self-generating growth, with a more equitable distribution of wealth through social development and efficiency improvements through technical innovation. However, the further round of international oil price increases, difficulties in keeping exports competitive and a poor harvest brought about negative growth of 5.2 per cent in 1980. The perceived need for a reappraisal of economic management was reflected in the current Fifth Plan, which came into operation in 1982.

World Bank figures suggest that between 1960 and 1979 only three other countries (Japan, Singapore and Romania) grew faster than South Korea. The first three Plans all achieved average real GNP annual growth rates above those actually planned (respectively achieving 7.9, 9.7 and 10.2 per cent), but the Fourth Plan, although projected at 9.2 per cent, could only achieve 5.7 per cent. Partly because of the uneven development in the agricultural sector, one characteristic of this continuous high average growth rate was a certain irregularity; on occasions the GNP growth rates as much as doubled or halved from year to year, creating a highly unstable situation for both investors and consumers.

It was the sense of competition, as North Korea was winning the developmental race in the 1950s and Japan was taking off in the early 1960s, that inspired a consensus in the South that development was essential. As even his political opponents have admitted, President Park was able to instil in the Korean people a positive attitude of 'we can do it'. In general, the population were persuaded to make sacrifices in the long-term national interest.

Under Park, the government administration was reorganized on lines which drew no little inspiration from the military backgrounds of the president and his immediate colleagues. The Economic Planning Board (EPB), established in 1961, took over the role of economic overlord (to a degree that its Japanese equivalent, the Economic Planning Agency, never has) and, although in recent years the Ministry of Commerce and Industry has grown in stature, the EPB remains the single most important organ of government. It is represented in the cabinet by the deputy prime minister and has a direct input into all the decision-making by the other economic ministries.

(b)   The government/business partnership
Public expenditure has been comparatively small in terms of GNP for a developing country (only 19 per cent in 1979), and the government has not owned major industries; but it has certainly

directed them. The degree of government intervention in the economy has clearly varied over time, but under Park, who drew lessons from the Japanese model, government officials worked closely with business leaders in giving strategic guidance for industrial development. Perhaps the government's most significant instrument at the microeconomic level has been the supply of preferential credit; control of the financial sector has been possible through government ownership of all the major banks. Since the Korean government is less dependent on business for political support than its Japanese equivalent, the system appeared to be much more officially directed 'from the top down'. However, the Park government encouraged the growth of quasi-governmental organizations, such as KOTRA (the Korea Trade Promotion Corporation) and KTA (the Korea Traders Association), which became part of the formal framework within which business could interact with government. More informal methods derived from the nature of Korean society, through family, alumni and other personal relationships; business leaders have been able to lobby for and against policies via the informal face-to-face relationships within the elite.

The Park government encouraged the growth of the *chaebol* (company groups), which extended their influence throughout the economy. According to one survey, in 1983 the twenty *chaebol* groups contributed, in value-added terms, the equivalent of 50 per cent of South Korea's total production of goods and services. The South now has ten companies in the *Fortune* list of the top 500 non-US companies, as many as Italy. However, few *chaebol* groups have holding company structures with a proper legal identity, many are still under direct family control with cross-directorships and cross-shareholdings, most are heavily reliant on borrowing (Hyundai had a debt ratio of 312 per cent in 1983), and they seem preoccupied with sales at the expense of wafer-thin profits. They have spread their interests across a large number of industries, not always wisely, preferring to take over older companies or found new ones rather than go in for sub-contracting chains on the Japanese scale. Several of them have associated general trading companies – set up in 1975 and modelled closely on the Japanese *sogoshosha* – which have come to dominate exporting to the extent that in 1984 the nine designated general trading companies were responsible for 48 per cent of South Korean exports. Doubts about the pervasive influence of these *chaebol* on the economy led to a reassessment under the Chun administration which will be discussed later.

(c) The educated population

The influx of refugees from the North during the Korean War brought the South's population to 21 million in 1953; by 1985, the population had grown to 41 million. In the 1950s, population growth was around 3 per cent per annum, but by the 1980s it had slowed to around 1.5 per cent, partly because of the natural passing of the post-Korean War baby boom and more recently because of increased family planning and abortions. With an average population density in 1985 of 408 persons per square kilometre, South Korea is now one of the most densely populated countries in the Third World. The mountainous nature of the country, which leaves less than a quarter of it cultivatable, means not only that there is little prospect of supporting the population through primary sector activity, but also that there has been an increasing tendency for the rural population to move to the cities. The rate of growth of this movement has been less pronounced since the early 1970s, after serious efforts were made by the government to improve rural conditions, but over 65 per cent of the population now live in cities, 24 per cent of them in Seoul, which had a population of over 9.5 million according to the 1985 official census. At currently projected rates of growth the total South Korean population will reach 45 million by 1991 and 50 million by the year 2000.

As a result of this population growth, increases in the size of the workforce since 1965 have been high, and in the first half of the 1970s, as the post-Korean War youth came of age, the average annual increase of 4 per cent was just over double that of the population increase. However, since then workforce growth rates have gradually declined and in 1982 they actually dropped below the population growth rate.

The structure and characteristics of this rapidly growing workforce have altered during the last two decades, reflecting changes in the strength of different sectors of the economy, increasing urbanization, and the wider availability of education. Agriculture's share of the GNP has dropped from 46 per cent in 1962 to 15 per cent in 1985, while that of manufacturing has expanded from a meagre 10 per cent to 32 per cent during the same period (with light industries representing 14 per cent and heavy and chemical industries the remaining 18 per cent). The service sector has grown less dramatically, rising from 44 to 53 per cent. In employment terms the shift has been more pronounced, with agricultural employment dropping from 61 per cent in 1962 to 25 per cent in 1985, and manufacturing rising from 8 to 23 per cent and the services from 29 to 45 per cent over the same period. Thus, the manufacturing and service industries were able to absorb not only large absolute increases in the economically active population, but also an estimated one million workers who shifted from agriculture to other employment during the 1976–80 period. Unemployment is more difficult to measure because the official statistics do not fully allow for seasonal fluctuations in the non-farm economy, but, officially, the rate dropped from 8 per cent in 1963 to only 3 per cent in 1978, although it did rise again slightly after that and was just over 4 per cent in 1985.

The Koreans have always respected education, and the general level of education of the labour force has been gradually rising since the 1950s. Primary schooling is free, but anything after that has involved considerable costs to the families – one estimate has calculated that 40 per cent of an average family's income is required to pay for a graduate student's education. The government endeavoured to make all middle-school education free by 1985, but that target has not been attained. Yet illiteracy has been virtually eliminated. By 1979, 93 per cent of those leaving primary school went on to middle school, and 81 per cent of those leaving middle school went on to high school. It is probable, however, that while the quantity of schooling has increased the quality has not significantly; indeed, in terms of pupil/teacher ratios, middle schools have actually deteriorated. Nevertheless, the rising level of education is reflected in the labour force; for example, the percentage of new worker entrants into the manufacturing sector with an educational attainment over the middle-school level increased between 1978 and 1982 from 29 to 40 per cent. However, the rising expectations are not always met with job opportunities, and less than half of the 113,000 spring 1985 college graduates were able to start immediately in jobs. The government is well aware of the potential effects of their discontent.

The rote-learning type of education that Korean children receive is conducive to producing an efficient and well-qualified labour force – though it is probably less suited to producing managers with initiative – and industrial productivity has shown a long-term upward trend despite substantial annual fluctuations, averaging around 10 per cent between 1970 and 1979 (one percentage point higher for the manufacturing sector alone) and 11.7 per cent for the 1980–3 period.

Real wages have also been increasing, except in 1980, when they recorded negative growth (though not quite to the same extent as productivity). In the manufacturing sector real wages increased annually by only 6 per cent on average in 1972–5, went up by 16 per cent in 1976–9 (when high wage increases were given to avoid labour troubles during a period of shortage of skilled labour), but fell back to only 2.5 per cent in 1980–3. South Korean development has been characterized by a degree of income equality not always seen in developing economies, with managers and administrators in 1982 receiving only 2.5 per cent higher salaries than the average wage for the whole economy. However, there are disparities between urban and rural incomes, which cause resentment. Moreover, female workers, who now represent 38 per cent of the workforce, suffer from discriminatory wage levels, averaging only about half the rates paid to their male colleagues. This low wage level is of crucial significance in certain export industries, such as textiles and electronics, in which the percentage of female workers is much higher. In fact, it has been argued that there are two types of South Korean export industry: one, the labour-intensive industries such as textiles and electronics, which employ predominantly women; the other, industries such as shipbuilding and steel, in which competitive advantage is probably gained more by efficient capital equipment than by low labour costs.

(d) Interaction with the international economy

Although recent studies have suggested that the origins of South Korean growth in the 1960s were largely domestic – even in 1970 exports accounted for only 14 per cent of GNP, having provided less than 30 per cent of the annual GNP increases during the 1960s – export growth became the most rapid element.[5] South Korean export growth averaged 34 per cent in real terms in the decade 1960–9 and 25 per cent in 1970–9. No other country in the world was able to sustain an annual export growth rate of over 20 per cent throughout those two decades. In the 1970s, the export of manufactured goods very clearly became the moving force behind economic development, so that by 1980 exports totalled $17.5 bn, the equivalent of 40 per cent of GNP.

Along with the growth of export volume, there has been a fundamental transformation of the commodity structure of Korean exports. The share of primary products, from agriculture, fishery and mining, declined from 73 per cent in 1962 to 7 per cent in 1980. Manufactured exports correspondingly increased from 27 to 93 per cent. At the same time, the share of light manufactured goods in total exports decreased during the 1970s, particularly after the government-sponsored expansion of heavy and chemical industries in 1973–4. In 1982, the value of heavy and chemical exports actually surpassed that of light manufactured goods.

However, South Korean exports are heavily concentrated on a few commodities; the ten major goods accounted for over 80 per cent of total exports in 1980. Textiles alone accounted for 29 per cent, followed by ships, steel, footwear and machinery. Moreover, exports were directed at a limited number of markets, with two-thirds of exports in the early 1980s going to the industrialized countries, and with Japan and the United States taking more than half. These two countries are similarly dominant among import sources.

The growth of exports has been accompanied by a growth of imports; the import component of exported goods reached 30 per cent in value during 1980. South Korea is poor in natural resources and energy, and in the 1950s and 1960s imports mainly satisfied the demand for the raw materials and capital goods needed for domestic consumption and production activities. But in the 1970s, the demand for materials and intermediate goods for the production of export goods increased in line with the rapid growth of exports. Energy imports nevertheless still remained important, and in 1979 imported oil provided 63 per cent of domestic energy consumption. This made the economy vulnerable to the oil shocks, and annual current-account deficits of over $4 bn were recorded for 1979–81.

With the sole exception of 1977, South Korea has suffered from a balance-of-payments deficit every year since the Korean War. Given the relatively low level of domestic savings and the need to cover the current-account deficits, the Park government sought a means of financing development spending. It decided to use foreign loans rather than direct foreign investment. By 1979, total external debt had reached $20 bn, generating a debt service ratio of 19 per cent.

When imported oil prices increased in 1979–80, the government decided on an intensified export offensive, but based primarily on *won* devaluation and depreciation in order to maintain price competitiveness. This combination of problems was compounded by a poor harvest following a drought and by political uncertainty. In 1980, negative GNP growth was recorded for the first time.

The Fifth Five-Year Plan and its successor
The Chun administration endeavoured first of all to stabilize the economy, by reducing inflationary pressures (the consumer price index rose by 30 per cent in 1980) and controlling all major cost factors such as wages and interest. The high priority placed on stabilization was reflected in the Five-Year Plan adopted in 1982. Critical of economic policies under Park, it talked about a 'changing role' for the government *vis-à-vis* private economic activities. In general terms this implied that the government would become less interventionist so as to allow more private sector initiative and efficiency, though it would play a larger role in social (it was the first plan to include the word 'social' in the title), technological and manpower development. Exports would remain the leading edge of growth, but the domestic market would become more exposed to foreign competition, including direct foreign investment.

The important goal of price stability was achieved; inflation dropped to 7 per cent in 1982 and 3 per cent in 1983, at which level it has roughly remained ever since. During the 1970s, South Korea had paid for its high growth with high inflation (in only one year was there a single-digit inflation rate). This had adverse social consequences, hitting low-income groups the hardest; it also eroded industrial competitiveness and encouraged speculation in assets such as real estate, which were considered inflation-proof, rather than productive investment. Chun, who considers inflation to have been one of the major factors that undermined Park's support, has been particularly concerned to keep it down.

However, progress in deregulation and liberalization of the economy has been slower, partly because it was a longer-term objective, but partly also because there has been significant opposition both within and outside government to some of the liberalization proposals. In addition, external economic factors have played a delaying role in several instances. The government has endeavoured to undertake reforms in three particular areas.

First, *financial liberalization* in order to nurture competition, by denationalizing the banks, liberalizing the interest rate structure and allowing greater participation by foreign banks. The government moved to divest its equity share in the five major banks, though the Ministry of Finance has retained supervisory responsibility for all commercial banks. A number of loan scandals erupted in 1982 and 1983 as a consequence of the unofficial 'kerb' market for loans – often at usurious interest rates – which had grown up to cater for the needs of companies hampered by government-instituted credit-rationing. These scandals underlined the need for governmental efforts to open up the financial system. Two cases in particular embarrassed the government: the 'Mrs Chang affair' in 1982, which involved the aunt of the president, and the Myongsong real estate group affair, after which a former cabinet minister under Chun was arrested. The government has tried hard to reduce the kerb market by raising official interest rates to a more realistic level and by boosting investment through increased lending by commercial banks to certain target areas, such as export-related facilities and small and medium-sized businesses (for example, Korean banks are required to allocate 35 per cent of new loans to firms in this latter category).

In 1981, the government committed itself to a gradual liberalization of the capital market. It chose 1990 as the target date for complete openness to foreign capital and for allowing Koreans to invest in foreign securities. The first stage, now in effect, has allowed foreigners to buy Korean securities indirectly, through the medium of managed trust funds (these now number six, but the total capitalization is only $240 million), and has let foreign brokerage firms establish a presence in Korea, although they cannot yet transact domestic business. The decision in November 1985 to allow foreigners to hold convertible bonds issued by major Korean companies was an encouraging sign, but the already cautious pace of the liberalization plan has suffered from slippages in time, since the planned commitment to allow foreigners to deal directly in Korean equity in 1985 is not to be honoured until October 1987.

Second, a *realignment of industrial policy*. Towards the end of the inflation of the 1970s, wage increases and oil price rises helped to erode the competitiveness of the capital-intensive heavy and chemical industries, which had been encouraged after 1973. High-cost, poor-quality goods were being produced by sectors in which capacity utilization was low. As a result, some major heavy industries were streamlined, mergers on a product-line basis were arranged, and the focus of preferential credit and tax treatment was shifted towards the promotion of high-technology and skill-intensive activities. Energy conservation measures were taken, and a long-term energy programme for reducing dependence on oil and increasing nuclear power and natural gas supplies was instituted. The government also tried to rationalize the activities of the *chaebol* groups by encouraging better financial structures, forcing them to shed superfluous subsidiaries, and replacing diversification with specialization. The *chaebol* have proved resistant, so probably with the intention of giving a message to the other groups, the government actually declined to come to the rescue of the eighth largest *chaebol*, Kukje-ICC, when it exhausted its credit lines in February 1985.

Successive South Korean governments have preferred Korean firms to pursue technology through licensing agreements, but the realization that certain high technology might only be available through associated direct foreign investment has been a factor leading the Chun administration to relax the rules. Thus, net flows of foreign investment, which totalled only $1.2 bn for 1962–81, reached $875 million during 1982–4 alone. New administrative measures in July 1984 reversed the previous system, so that now all areas are open to foreign investment except those specified on the negative list (those sectors still closed include newspapers, the postal service and agriculture). As a result, new foreign investment in 1985 amounted to $532m, 88 per cent of which came from US and Japanese sources. Foreign investors, nevertheless, still complain about the bureaucratic implementation of the new regulations, difficulties with profit repatriation and the lack of protection for intellectual property.

Technology transfer has become one of the key issues in South Korea's negotiations with its trading partners, above all with the Japanese, who have shown a marked reluctance to provide the requested technology, not least because of their fear of the 'boomerang effect' of aiding potential rivals who might then make inroads into their domestic market. The South Koreans have shown an ability to play off foreign rivals against one another in order to get some necessary technology – for example, the Europeans and the Japanese over equipment for the Pohang Iron and Steel Company's second integrated steel mill. However, they are well aware of the deficiencies in the in-house research and development of Korean companies. In 1984, Korean manufacturers' research and development expenditure averaged 1.3 per cent of total turnover as compared with over 3 per cent for US and German companies; accordingly, the government is boosting funds available for technology development, with the aim of making research and development investment equivalent to 2 per cent of GNP in 1986.

Third, *import liberalization*, to force domestic industries to become more efficient when faced with foreign competition. The import liberalization ratio has risen from 69 per cent in 1980 to 84 per cent in 1985, and is due to reach 91 per cent by the end of 1986. Although some domestic producers are being given temporary tariff protection, the average tariff rate is to be reduced to 17 per cent by 1988. The government has utilized the advance-notice system of liberalization to give indigenous producers and importers several years for adjustment. The lowest ratios for liberalization are still in the primary products sector (imports of agricultural goods are politically sensitive, especially since the ruling DJP relies heavily on the rural vote) and in the miscellaneous manufactured goods sector (where it is felt necessary to protect the small and medium-sized firms), but the highest are in the chemical and iron and steel sectors, for which scarce raw materials and intermediate goods are essential. It is the sectors covering machinery and electrical equipment which are set to undergo the most rapid liberalization from 1986 to 1988. Yet, for foreign suppliers, one perceived need is for the reduction of the government's use of 'surge' and import surveillance measures to restrict import of products that rise dramatically.

The targeted ratios for import liberalization listed above have in fact been revised upwards as part of a general revision, made in late 1983, to the current Five-Year Plan. The revised plan raised the targets for domestic savings and export growth and took as its key objective the elimination of the current-account deficit during 1986. In macroeconomic terms, there were two motives behind revising the plan in such a manner. One was to extend stabilization efforts based on the sharp drop in inflation in 1982–3; but the more important one was to restrain the foreign debt, which had grown from $20.5 bn in

1979 to $40.1 bn by the end of 1983. Only by maintaining export growth in real terms were those debts able to be serviced.

The level of external debt has continued to rise, though less dramatically than in the 1979–83 period, to reach $46.7 bn (or 56 per cent of GNP) at the end of 1985. Although South Korea is the fourth largest debtor in the world after Brazil, Mexico and Argentina, it has generally been able to obtain favourable borrowing terms. It continues to borrow about $6 bn a year, but the government has been using an increasing proportion of this to refinance existing loans and to extend the maturity structure of outstanding debt. Indeed, the debt service ratio, excluding short-term debt repayment, has risen only slightly, from 18.2 per cent in 1975 to 20.5 per cent in 1984. The massive growth in the external debt has left the Chun administration vulnerable to criticism from the political opposition, not least because traditionally Koreans do not like to live beyond their means, and being in debt to foreigners, above all, is disturbing to a nationalistic people. Therefore, the government's overriding aim is to eliminate the current-account deficit by the end of 1986, thereby eradicating the primary cause of the buildup in external debt.

The Korean planners have helped to generate export growth by trying to maintain price competitiveness by allowing the *won* to depreciate against the US dollar. This has increased exports to the United States, which in 1985 took 35 per cent of total South Korean exports as compared with 26 per cent in 1980, but has made the South Korean economy even more vulnerable to any slowdown in the US economy, such as that which occurred in 1985. The softening of export demand imposed financial strains on the major exporting industries. It has also led to the growing politicization of US-Korean trade relations; the Koreans have reacted strongly against some of the protectionist measures proposed by US politicians during 1985–6.

Real GNP growth fell in 1985 to 5.1 per cent from the 1984 figure of 8.4 per cent, and, in dollar (but not in *won*) terms, per capita GNP actually fell slightly. However, in late 1985 to early 1986, a number of other external changes seemed on balance to favour the South Korean economy and make it likely that in 1986 a current-account surplus would be achieved. First, the *won's* significant depreciation against the yen (the *won* fell 42 per cent against the yen between September 1985 and July 1986) encouraged Korean exports (even if importers had to pay more for Japanese capital goods). Second, with much of the foreign debt pegged to US prime and Euromarket rates, a one-point decline in international interest rates could save $350m. Third, as oil prices fell, the losses in the invisible account through a reduction in earnings from construction activity in the Middle East have been more than compensated for by savings on energy import costs (oil alone represents about 18 per cent of the total import bill), even though petrol consumption has increased slightly with lower prices. Korean economists estimate a benefit of around $150m a year to the balance of payments for each dollar drop in the price of a barrel of oil. Projections for 1986 GNP growth have now been revised upwards to 10 per cent; exports are expected to reach $33 bn.

During 1985–6, the government has been preparing the Sixth Five-Year Plan (1987–91), and the projections have been revised upwards in successive drafts as the country's economic performance has improved during 1986. The adjusted projections announced in July 1986 are shown in Table 3.2.

Table 3.2 Growth of the South Korean economy (actual and projected) during the Fifth and Sixth Five-Year Plans

	1982	1985	1991
Population (million)	39.3	41.0	44.1
GNP ($ bn)	69.4	83.1	160.6
Per capita GNP ($)	1,773	2,032	3,650
Exports ($ bn)	21.9	30.3	53.1
Imports ($ bn)	24.3	31.0	48.8
Current account ($ bn)	−2.7	−0.9	3.0
External debt ($ bn)	37.1	46.7	51.4

Sources: Bank of Korea, Seoul, *Monthly Statistical Bulletin* (various issues), and *Korea Herald*, 6 July 1986.

During the period of the Sixth Plan, real GNP is forecast to grow at an average of 7.4 per cent per year to reach $160 bn at current prices or $3,650 per capita by 1991. Exports are expected to grow at 8.8 per cent per annum and imports to increase less rapidly so as to allow the trade surplus to reach $4.3 bn and the current-account surplus $3 bn by 1991. By 1988, the import liberalization ratio will reach 95 per cent, but important categories such as automobiles, agricultural products and some consumer goods will still be subject to quantitative restriction. Tariff rates are being lowered, but on certain 'non-essential' goods are likely to remain high. The government is aware that South Korea is losing its comparative advantage to other Third World countries in traditional labour-intensive industries, and therefore aims gradually to phase out 'smokestack' industries and place priority on such sectors as machinery, electronics and automobiles. The four major *chaebol* are being encouraged to invest $1 bn over the next four years in research into and production of high-grade semi-conductors, personal computers and telecommunications.

As a result of the expected increases in domestic savings, direct foreign investment (which will supply 12 per cent of foreign capital inflow instead of the current 3 per cent) and foreign assets, the foreign debt total will reach only $51.4 bn by 1991 (a politically more acceptable figure than the initially announced $61.4 bn), equivalent to 33 per cent of GNP (as compared with 57 per cent in 1985). The Korea Development Institute actually projects that by 1998 South Korea will turn into a net creditor country.

Although a small but efficient government is the motto for those officials involved in drafting the new plan, the government's control of the day-to-day running of the economy has been only gradually reduced during the current plan, and even Korean scholars remain sceptical about how far the market will be able to function freely under the new plan. A number of external and internal factors could act to keep performance below some of the ambitious medium-term projections and constrain moves to genuine economic liberalization: a less favourable international trading environment as oil prices rise again in 1987–8 and protectionism in South Korea's main markets increases; financial stress in the corporate and banking sectors as industrial policy changes; and, finally, strains in the political and social fabric as resentment at economic and social inequalities increasingly finds expression in criticism of the stunted political growth. Nevertheless, South Korea has surprised observers in the past with its resilience in the face of economic difficulties; it may well do so again.

The North Korean economy

North Korea, like its southern counterpart, has managed to trans-form a backward economy ravaged by war into a predominantly industrial one, but, even though both countries share a commitment to planning for economic development, their economies have increasingly diverged.

Since North Korea ceased publishing comprehensive annual economic statistics in the mid-1960s, it has been difficult to measure and compare the progress of its economy. Published data tend to indicate only percentages of change over a long time, with no solid baseline. The South Korean National Unification Board's estimates give North Korean GNP in 1983 as $14.47 bn, which, given a population of 18.9 million people, means a per capita GNP level of only $765. Although the World Bank no longer provides these figures (for 1979 it suggested $1,130 for per capita GNP as compared with North Korean claims of $1,920), the placing of North Korea in its listings suggests a significantly higher per capita GNP than the South Korean estimate, though still below South Korea's own level. Until about 1974 North Korean per capita GNP was probably higher than the equivalent figure in the South.

Aided by a considerable amount of economic assistance from the Soviet Union, China and East European countries, the goal of restoring the North Korean economy after the Korean War to prewar levels was attained by 1956. The economy displayed impress-ive rates of growth during the second half of the 1950s, particularly during the period of the First Five-Year Plan, dating from 1957 to 1960 (because it was achieved ahead of schedule in the manufactur-ing sector), when GNP annual growth rates averaged 21 per cent. The North Koreans initially patterned their economic system and central planning closely on the Soviet model, with direct politico-administrative regulation of the macro- and microeconomic proces-ses of production, distribution, exchange and accumulation. Alhough this played a positive role in the early stages of industrialization, the economic costs of a heavily 'statist' mode of development have become increasingly apparent. In the 1950s, rapid industrialization was the keynote; heavy industry was designated the leading sector of development, with moderate growth allowed for in light industry and agriculture to meet consumer demand. By 1958, the socialization of the North Korean economy across all sectors was deemed complete. However, the leadership became increasingly attracted to China's ideological zeal and, in 1959, the year after the Chinese Great Leap Forward, the North Koreans introduced their own movement to stimulate productivity – the *chollima*, or flying horse, movement.

However, the over-confidence and over-zealousness derived from the progress of the 1950s hampered realistic planning for the First Seven-Year Plan, which, due to slowdowns in growth rates and reverses in production, had to be extended for three years, effectively becoming a ten-year plan from 1961 to 1970. Average annual growth rates for industrial output declined from 36 per cent during the First Five-Year Plan (1957–60) to 12 per cent during the First Seven-Year Plan (1961–70), as compared with the target of 18 per cent. Bottlenecks had arisen in certain sectors, and during the Six-Year Plan (1971–76) some changes were made to development strategy. The most significant, apparently in part resulting from the impressions gained by North Koreans visiting the South for the Red Cross talks in 1972, was the launching of a large-scale programme for purchasing foreign plant and technology and expanding foreign trade. These changes had beneficial effects on industrial productivity, and the average annual growth rate of industrial output reached 16 per cent in the 1971–6 period (and the Plan was announced as being fulfilled sixteen months ahead of schedule); but the rising prices of oil and some other raw materials, combined with a drop in the prices of some North Korean non-ferrous metal exports, brought about a balance-of-payments problem. North Korea's failure to pay its trade bills during this period and the consequent attempts to reschedule its debts have remained a continuing irritant in its trade with non-communist countries.

In common with other developing countries, including South Korea, there has been structural transformation of the economy as development has proceeded. The share of agriculture in the total national product has decreased rapidly, while that of industry has correspondingly grown. The number of farm households and the farming population have decreased, although productivity has increased to the extent that self-sufficiency in food was achieved around 1974. Latest figures suggest that agricultural production is equivalent to 24 per cent of GNP and non-agricultural production to 76 per cent.

A year of 'readjustment' was allowed before the Second Seven-Year Plan began in 1978. The main emphasis of the Plan (1978–84) was placed on strengthening the socialist economy by means of the 'three great revolutions', that is, self-reliance (*juche*), modernization and 'scientification' (which to all intents and purposes is the same as modernization). Self-reliance means developing the economy through domestic resources and technology; modernization means updating management, and automating and mechanizing all the means of production. At the October 1980 Sixth KWP Congress, 'ten great goals' for the economy to achieve during the 1980s were adopted. In the main sectors of the economy, that meant emphasis on hydroelectric power and coal as sources of energy, on steel and non-ferrous metals in heavy industry, on grain and land reclamation in agriculture, on textiles in light industry and on dried marine products in fisheries.

The results of that Plan (1978–84) were announced in February 1985. It was said to be over-fulfilled in terms of growth of gross industrial output value, which averaged 12.2 per cent per annum. The major tasks of doubling manufacturing output, of almost doubling the national income, and of raising grain production to an annual total of ten million tons, were said to have been achieved. The Six-Year Plan and the Second Seven-Year Plan periods have therefore seen targets apparently fulfilled by slight margins (by contrast with the obvious failure of the First Seven-Year Plan), though these successes might just reflect more realistic targets.

As the 1980 goals and the Second Seven-Year Plan suggest, there are certain problems hampering the pace of North Korean economic development. Although population growth is averaging around 2.2 per cent annually, North Korea is a relatively labour-scarce country (particularly by Asian standards). The substantial diversion of manpower into the armed forces does not help. Difficulties in both the quantity and quality of workers were clearly behind the Plan's endeavours to improve the comprehensive eleven-year compulsory education system and to train more technicians and specialists, particularly in engineering. The failure to announce industrial figures for all of the intermediate years of the Plan suggests

39

considerable fluctuations in output. Poor transportation has imposed limitations on the supply of materials required by industry, and increases in cargo capacity and the electrification of railway lines are seen as key targets.

Industrial growth has also been affected by the inability of the energy and mining industries to supply the power and raw materials as fast as the manufacturing industry has needed them. Coal has been crucial, since more than two-thirds of the electric power is generated by coal-fired power stations. Soviet and Polish technicians have been involved in a major development of the Anju coalfield. Significantly, electric power, together with steel and non-ferrous metals, was one of the three industries not mentioned as having achieved the targets under the Second Seven-Year Plan.

Finally, the shortage of foreign currency, with Western credit virtually drying up after 1976 and a continuing balance-of-trade deficit, has restricted the import of Western technology and plant. After an agreement was reached with Japan, its largest foreign creditor, in 1979, North Korea began repayment of its debts, but from 1983 the payments again began to drop behind schedule. According to Japanese calculations, North Korea had an average annual trade deficit of \$250m from 1980 to 1984; in 1985 the deficit reached \$465m.[6]

The North Korean economic planners have to walk a delicate tightrope between the two goals of self-reliance and modernization, if the latter can only be achieved with modern technology from abroad. In recent years, therefore, there have been occasional signs that for all the rhetoric, self-reliance, in its practical application, not least in the area of foreign trade, has displayed a certain amount of flexibility. This has been the case not just in relation to the Soviet Union and China, which remain North Korea's main aid donors and trade partners (significantly, Soviet academics have been at some pains in recent years to emphasize that Soviet technical assistance has continued, even if at a far lower level than that of the 1950s – the Kimchaek Iron Works, which opened in 1983, is just one example);[7] it has been even more pronounced in relation to the West and international organizations. In 1980, North Korea applied to the United Nations Development Programme for assistance in developing ports and railways and the electronic industry; it received nearly \$9m. Of more significance was the announcement in September 1984 of a joint-venture law, which drew inspiration from similar legislation in China. Although North Korean officials initially implied that the new law was aimed primarily at European companies, the main emphasis recently has been on encouraging Japanese companies to invest. However, only two joint ventures have been agreed, one Japanese project for a department store (backed mainly by Koreans in Japan) and a French project to construct a hotel. The North has made hotel construction a priority (with capacity to be tripled to 30,000 beds by 1988) in part because of its desire to co-host the next Olympic Games, but also because Western tourists would be a new source of hard currency. Western companies have, however, remained unenthusiastic about joint ventures while the problem of outstanding debts from the 1970s remains unresolved.

Although Kim Il-sung told a Cuban newspaper in June 1985 that a new plan was being prepared, the delay in the announcement of the succeeding seven-year plan not only shows that problems still exist within the economy; it may also reflect divisions within the leadership about the extent to which new economic strategies should be employed. The importance of the economic policy debate, even though it is carried on mainly behind closed doors, can be judged from the domination of the last three meetings of the KWP Central Committee, since July 1984, by economic issues. One attempt at rationalization, presumably in preparation for the new plan, was the decision in November 1985 to reorganize thirteen ministries dealing with aspects of the economy into six commissions, which rank higher.

Since the 1960s, some other socialist countries have undertaken varying degrees of reform to incorporate market elements into their economies; the Yugoslav 'market socialism' and Hungarian 'administrative decentralized economy' are earlier examples, and China's 'four modernizations' is a more recent one. However, North Korea has, if anything, strengthened the role of central planning. There have been tentative efforts to modernize management and to deal with the conflicting needs for central planning and for local or personal initiative, but the North Korean economy remains a rigidly centralized one. Any significant change in economic policy poses presentational problems, for unlike Deng Xiaoping in China, who can claim to be pursuing new policies in order to overcome the failures of his predecessors, Kim does not want to undermine the prestige which he has invested in earlier policies.

Doubts must remain as to how long the reliance on revolutionary zeal and exhortations (currently the 'speed of the eighties') and other basically non-pecuniary incentives can continue. As President Kim implicitly admitted in his January 1980 New Year speech, by his references to the need 'to strengthen the ideological struggle against conservatism, passiveness, and fear of technology', the economy has been plagued by the problems of bureaucratism and lethargy.[8] In the early part of 1986, the North Korean media have felt it necessary to criticize those who are 'grumbling' about the lack of material benefits from economic progress. The rise of the new generation of technocrats mentioned in the previous chapter should influence economic strategies, but much depends on the results of the impending succession and on the younger Kim's attitudes to his father's rigid economic policies once he alone is in power. The fear that economic openness may bring unbearable political costs has been a strong disincentive to positive reform in the past; it may well prove so again.

4
THE NORTH-SOUTH BALANCE

The competition between North and South Korea for prestige and legitimacy is based on both economic and military power. Chapter 3 considered some of the sources of economic power in both countries, and noted that the balance is shifting increasingly in favour of the South. This chapter will consider the military dimension, as well as the competition in the diplomatic arena. It will also assess the state of the present intermittent North-South dialogue, as both sides manoeuvre for advantage.

The military balance

A precarious truce on the border has survived for more than 30 years. To borrow the phrase used by Leon Trotsky as long ago as 1918, it is 'neither war nor peace'. Bitter memories of the Korean War still play a dominating role in military strategy on the peninsula. Both sides are aware of the vulnerability of their capitals. In the North, most of the population and industrial centres are located within 200 miles of the border, and Pyongyang itself is only 90 miles away. The North Koreans cannot forget the US blanket-bombing during the Korean War, which reduced their major centres to rubble. In the South, however, the industrial and political nerve-centre of Seoul is only 30 miles away from the border; it is thus within range of North Korean artillery. It took the invading North Korean army in June 1950 only three days to reach Seoul; today it is only three minutes' flying time away if North Korean aircraft were to attack. The South Koreans, therefore, remain obsessed by the fear of a surprise strike across the border in the manner of the invasion of 1950.

If the US forces are excluded from the comparison, the balance in quantitative terms favours the North. According to statistics available from the International Institute for Strategic Studies, in 1985 the North Korean armed forces totalled 838,000 men (750,000 army, 53,000 air force and 35,000 navy personnel), while the South Korean armed forces totalled 598,000 men (520,000 army, 33,000 air force, 23,000 navy and 22,000 marines). Conscription lasts for two years in the South (where it is unpopular with students) and for five years in the North. North Korea is thought to have around four million people with some form of reserve or militia commitment through such organizations as the Workers-Farmers Red Guards and the Youth Red Guards. The balance in weaponry is set out in Table 4.1.

Table 4.1 The military balance on the Korean peninsular

Type of weapon	North Korea	South Korea
Tanks	3,425	1,200
Armoured personnel carriers	1,100	700
Artillery pieces	4,650 (up to 240mm)	3,000 (up to 203mm)
Anti-aircraft guns	8,000	500
Surface-to-surface missiles	54 (*FROG*)	12 (*Honest John*)
Surface-to-air missiles	an unknown number of SA-7s	210 (*HAWK* and *Nike Hercules*)
Combat aircraft	800 (160 MiG-21s and 20 Su-7s)	451 (260 F-5s)
Naval vessels	532 (20 submarines)	155 (no submarines)

Source: *The Military Balance 1985–1986* (London, International Institute for Strategic Studies, 1985)

The North Korean numerical superiority, however, does not mean qualitative advantage. Just over one-third of the North

Korean planes are outmoded MiG-15s and MiG-17s, and only the MiG-21s are equivalent to the South Korean F-5s. Both sides are trying to upgrade their capabilities in this area; the South Koreans are deploying F-16 fighters from the United States (12 during 1986 out of a total of 36 ordered), and the North is beginning to obtain MiG-23s from the Soviet Union (26 already deployed out of a possible total of 50). However, the older MiG-23s cannot match the F-16s. Similarly, the North's naval advantage is not as great as might be imagined at first; over three-quarters of its vessels are in fact fast-attack or landing craft. In terms of total tonnage, the South Korean navy is superior.

Despite the unreliability of officially published budgetary figures for military expenditure, it is possible to discern certain trends. In the 1950s, the North Koreans put more emphasis on economic reconstruction than on military expenditure (anyway Chinese troops remained in the North until 1958), but in the 1960s they began to encourage defence industries and 'self-reliance'. In the mid-1960s, military expenditure increased significantly, and reached around 30 per cent of total government expenditure for the second half of the decade. Coincident with the short-lived North-South dialogue, in 1972 military expenditure dropped to around 17 per cent of total government expenditure. As a percentage it has declined slightly since, though in absolute terms it has continued to increase steadily. The 1985 budget set expenditure at 3.9 bn NK *won* (approximately $4,196m).

The South Korean military buildup began at a later stage than in the North. Throughout the 1960s and early 1970s, defence expenditure averaged around 28 per cent of total government expenditure, but not until 1976 did the publicly acknowledged defence expenditures become greater in the South than in the North. Under the first force-improvement plan (1975–81), South Korean military expenditure rose to 33 per cent of total government expenditure in 1976, and has increased slowly ever since. Under the second force-improvement plan (1982–6), the defence budget by 1985 had reached 3,825 bn SK *won* (approximately $4,402m), which is equivalent to $109 per capita and 6 per cent of GNP. In per capita terms and in proportion to GNP, defence expenditure is significantly lower in the South than the North. Given the greater absolute value for defence expenditure in the South, however, US and South Korean analysts estimate that South Korea should be able to reach military parity with the North at the beginning of the 1990s if current trends are continued. In the meantime, in the South Koreans' view, a rough military balance on the peninsula is maintained by the US presence of 39,500 troops, 90 combat aircraft (including F-16s), and tactical nuclear weapons.

Both sides have been aiming to develop and manufacture more of their own military material. Until the mid-1970s, the North had been well ahead in the production of weapons, but the South has acquired considerable technological capability since then and, usually under licence from the United States, can now produce heavy equipment, such as tanks and destroyers, as well as small arms. Indeed, in September 1985, the first combat aircraft to be built in South Korea, the F-5M fighter-bomber, was unveiled (though locally produced parts accounted for only 23 per cent of the aircraft). It is perhaps a measure of its progress in military technology that South Korea is one of only two East Asian countries that have been invited to participate in the US Strategic Defence Initiative research programme. North Korea also produces destroyers, submarines and medium tanks. However, despite these advances, both are likely to remain dependent on military aid and purchases from their patron states and allies for obtaining the most sophisticated military technology.

North Korean military strategy still owes much to the 'four major military lines' announced at the KWP Central Committee plenum in December 1962: namely, the arming of the whole population, the fortification of the entire country, the training of all soldiers as a cadre force, and the modernization of all the armed forces. The first three themes in particular constituted elements of protracted warfare, involving ideological as well as military training. In the 1970s, however, while a significant buildup in conventional military forces did occur, and the size of the armed forces increased from 467,000 in 1974 to 838,000 men in 1985 (over the same period the South Korean armed forces actually decreased by 27,000 men), growing attention was paid to means of unconventional warfare. Three North Korean infiltration tunnels dug under the demilitarized zone (DMZ) were discovered, in 1974, 1975 and 1978; these could have been used for a surprise attack or for the infiltration of guerrilla or commando units. North Korea developed possibly the world's largest commando force – now believed to number around 80,000 men – trained to move swiftly through Korea's difficult terrain and inflict maximum damage in the South through guerrilla action. 1983 saw three attempted commando infiltrations into the South, and the North Koreans responsible for the bomb attack on the presidential party visiting Rangoon the same year came from that elite group. Finally, the purchase of 87 US-made *Hughes* helicopters (identical to South Korean models) through German and Hong Kong inter-mediaries in 1985 offers the North Koreans another opportunity to cause confusion in the South, possibly by landing troops in South Korean uniforms.

Analysis of North Korean capabilities and strategies is compli-cated by the low public visibility of the military (there have been no military parades since 1972), the construction of a large number of underground facilities (more than 100 fortresses which are believed to conceal weaponry and armoured transport have been constructed close to the DMZ), and the state of almost perpetual alert of the forces near to the DMZ (defectors to the South talk about continual rigorous guard duty and training). South Korean and US military analysts suggest that since the late 1970s North Korean strategy has been slowly moving away from a protracted conventional war towards planning for an attack to gain limited objectives. North Korea would launch a massive blitzkrieg, ideally breaking through to capture the psychologically and economically important area around Seoul, and would then halt and seek a political settlement on the basis of the altered military situation. It would aim to gain a decisive advantage within five to seven days of the commencement of the war. As evidence for this, the South Koreans argue that by the end of 1985 over 65 per cent of overall North Korean military strength was deployed in the front-line area, the front-line forces had been made more mechanized and two new air bases had been constructed in the vicinity of the DMZ. The North's continued stress on its military buildup, as well as its terrorist and infiltration activities (though as far as *detected* infiltration is concerned, the rate is lower now than in earlier decades), leave the South with just cause for concern.

The North Koreans claim that their military buildup is for defensive purposes. The annual US-South Korean joint military manoeuvres called 'Team Spirit', which are the largest carried out in the non-communist world, are consistently denounced as warmongering and as a threat to the North. In response to the 1984 exercise, the North Koreans actually put their troops on a special war-alert footing for as long as it lasted. Although the North Korean statements about an American threat contain a strong propaganda flavour, they can also be construed as reflecting a deep-seated anxiety (the North Koreans see the US intervention of 1950 as a demonstration of a willingness to commit aggression).

South Korean military strategy is based on the 1954 US-South Korean Mutual Defence Treaty, under which US forces are based in South Korea, mostly between the DMZ and Seoul, and, since 1973, on the concept of 'forward defence'. If the presence of US troops in the front line is insufficient to prevent a North Korean attack, then rather than fall back to Seoul, South Korean forces would actually move forward to counter-attack across the DMZ. The command-and-control arrangements in the South are complex, but operational control of most of the South Korean troops lies with the US Commander-in-Chief of the Combined Forces Command. This causes resentment among those South Korean officers who dislike being in a subordinate position in their own country. General Chun's use of certain South Korean forces for internal political purposes in December 1979 exposed some of the sensitivities within the US-South Korean military relationship.

Although President Chun has described the next three years as being the most likely for an attack from the North, it is not clear how far North Korea is genuinely taken as a direct military threat by the South. In one opinion survey taken among the South Korean elite in 1982, only 40 per cent replied that they thought Kim Il-sung would invade the South.[9] The relative optimism of those interviewed can perhaps be explained by a certain disillusionment with past government manipulation of relevant information about North Korea and by a trust in the current US administration's power and willingness to help.

Diplomatic competition

As long as both North and South Korea see each other as potential enemies, the military buildup is essentially a zero-sum game. A conspicuous buildup in military capability on one side, in order to bolster its sense of security, tends to undercut the security, perceived or real, of the other. The competition for diplomatic legitimacy, too, had all the elements of a zero-sum game in the 1950s and 1960s; since the early 1970s, however, this characteristic has become less prominent.

The competition for legitimacy derived from the manner of the birth of the two rival governments. South Korea was, in a sense, a creation of the United Nations: the UN General Assembly in December 1948 passed a resolution declaring the South Korean government to be a 'lawful' one, after elections had been held in the southern part of Korea under UN auspices in May of that year. The Soviet Union refused to allow UN-supervised elections in the North. One South Korean government after another has consistently maintained that it is the only lawful government in the whole of the Korean peninsula. For its part, the North Korean government, established after elections in the Soviet occupation zone in August 1948, has categorically rejected both South Korean claims to legitimacy and pro-South Korean resolutions at the United Nations.

As decolonization gathered pace in the 1960s and 1970s, the newly independent Third World countries became the target of North and South Korean diplomatic lobbying. In January 1963, only 15 countries had full ambassadorial relations with the North as compared with 56 with the South; yet, by January 1977, 93 had ties with the North as compared with 96 with the South. The period 1973–5 proved particularly productive for the North, for it succeeded in establishing diplomatic relations with six West European countries (all five Scandinavian countries and Portugal), in gaining admission to the World Health Organization (thereby gaining permanent-observer status at the United Nations), in being admitted to the Non-Aligned Movement (NAM) while South Korea was not, and, finally, in 1975, in scoring a symbolic victory when the UN General Assembly passed two contradictory resolutions, one favourable to South Korea, the other, for the first time ever, supportive of the North. In June 1973, accepting the inevitable, President Park's government officially dropped its insistence on its version of the West German 'Hallstein doctrine', under which it refused to deal with any country that recognized North Korea. The South Korean government announced that it would not oppose North Korea's participation in international organizations of which it was already a member, and, for the first time, suggested simultaneous entry of both North and South into the United Nations as separate states.

President Kim immediately responded by rejecting the proposal for simultaneous admission to the United Nations; from his viewpoint, such a step would effectively freeze the status quo, so perpetuating the division of the peninsula. Nevertheless, although the North has been reluctant to allow its closest allies to endorse anything resembling a 'two Koreas' policy (as will be shown in the next chapter), it has been more flexible with regard to Third World countries. As of 1985, 101 countries had relations with North Korea and 125 with the South, and as many as 69 countries had relations with both.

In the 1980s, South Korea has diversified its diplomatic approaches to the Third World, employing what has been described as 'invitational diplomacy', and it has been rewarded with several symbolic victories over the North. President Chun visited the then five countries of ASEAN (the Association of South-East Asian Nations) in June/July 1981 and, although four of them have diplomatic relations with the North, they expressed their support for South Korean unification proposals. The President also visited four African countries (Kenya, Gabon, Nigeria and Senegal) in August 1982 and Burma in October 1983 at the start of an abortive South Asian/Australasian tour. The almost universal disapprobation of the North after the Rangoon attack, particularly when Burma, a country with impeccable non-aligned credentials, not only broke off diplomatic relations but actually withdrew recognition, left North Korea isolated. A number of countries imposed temporary diplomatic sanctions, two countries suspended diplomatic relations and three countries (including Pakistan) recognized the South for the first time.

In addition, President Chun has secured visits from foreign leaders such as Japanese Prime Minister Yasuhiro Nakasone, Pope John Paul II and President Reagan, as well as from a number of West European prime ministers. South Korea has also succeeded in hosting a number of international meetings – the Inter-parliamentary Union convention in 1983, the annual International Monetary Fund/World Bank conference in 1985, the Asian Games in 1986 and, most significantly, the 1988 Olympic Games – which could not have been secured without significant numerical support from Third World nations.

For a mixture of economic and political reasons, President Chun has sought to improve his links with other Asian Pacific countries, and, conscious of the embryonic discussions, mainly among academics and businessmen, in the late 1970s and early 1980s about some form of Pacific Community, he has become one of the few government leaders in the region to endorse such ideas openly. When he met Australian Prime Minister Malcolm Fraser in May 1982, he floated the idea of a regular summit, open to leaders of all Asian Pacific countries, to discuss economic and social questions. Although the response from the region was muted, Chun felt committed enough to the idea to raise it again officially when he visited Japan in September 1984.

North Korea has its own version of 'invitational diplomacy' and has had some successes in hosting international meetings, notably NAM conferences dealing with food and agriculture, in 1981, and with news agencies, in 1982, but it has failed to secure an NAM general meeting or any other large-scale international meeting. Moreover, at the 1983 NAM summit in New Delhi, North Korea failed to get a clause calling for the withdrawal of foreign troops from the Korean peninsula included in the final communiqué. However, it may find more support for its resolutions as Zimbabwe succeeds India as the NAM lead country. Zimbabwe is one of a number of countries that have received North Korean weaponry or military training; arms sales on the scale of the reportedly $800m deal with Iran in 1982 are an important source of foreign currency. North Korean diplomats, however, have been expelled from a number of countries because of their involvement in illicit arms sales, drug smuggling and bribery.

The intensity of this diplomatic competition in the international arena is unlikely to decline in the near future, especially in view of the approach of the 1988 Olympics. It may also continue to create confusion in the minds of some Third World leaders courted by both sides; when President Chun stepped down from his aircraft in Gabon in 1982, he was greeted by the local official band playing the North Korean national anthem!

The North-South dialogue

Both Koreas have embraced national unification as a major, sometimes the major, strategic policy objective. The division of the country and the internecine war which followed have left a traumatic legacy for the Korean people; South Korean television conducted an emotional series of programmes in 1983 to reunite families separated during the war and scattered throughout the South. Yet, until the current series of dialogues began in 1984, there had been no official or substantial relations between the two states north and south of the 38th parallel apart from brief dialogues in 1972–3 and 1979–80. Even now there are no direct exchanges of postal or telephonic communication (except for an official hot line between the two governments) and no crossings of the border by individuals (except for a limited number of officials involved in talks and the one limited 'separated family visit' in September 1985).

North Korean unification policy has been more clearly enunciated and more doggedly pursued than in the South. Of course, the tenacity of the desire to achieve the elusive goal of unification is a by-product of the longevity of Kim Il-sung. His statements suggest that all North Korean endeavours should be devoted to the overriding goals of 'liberating' the South Korean people from the twin shackles of 'US imperialism' and 'fascist repression' and reunifying the peninsula. When answering questions from a Japanese journalist in July 1985, Kim argued that the North had 'neither the intention nor the capability of invading the South', but added that 'we must reunify the nation in our generation at all costs'.[10]

In the decade after the Korean War, unification was de-emphasized as North Korea concentrated on economic recovery, but since the early 1960s, when Kim enunciated his 'three revolutionary forces' theory, unification has remained a salient issue in the North. The three components of his strategy are: building a powerful revolutionary base in the North, fostering the revolutionary capability of the South (a Revolutionary Party for Reunification, to be based in the South, was founded in 1964), and strengthening international revolutionary forces, with the aim of isolating the United States and compelling it to withdraw its forces from the peninsula. In reality, the strict anti-communist laws in the South have prevented the RPR from being anything other than an organized party in name only – its radio broadcasts from the North rather than inside the South – and, apart from momentary hesitation after Jimmy Carter became president, the Americans have shown little sign of substantial withdrawal.

Kim's vision of unification, expressed in slightly different forms over the last two and half decades, has come to be a confederal republic. At the Sixth KWP Congress in October 1980, Kim expressed this vision in its most refined form, as the Democratic Confederal Republic of Koryo (DCRK). Foreshadowing what later became popularized in China as 'one country, two systems' (a phrase first used by Deng Xiaoping in 1982), two separate social and governmental systems would coexist, for the foreseeable future, under the rubric of the DCRK and its 'supreme national confederal assembly'. Economic, cultural, and military collaboration between North and South would cover a wide spectrum, but there would be only one 'national army', unified foreign and defence policies, and central direction of the important aspects of administration. The newest element was the apparent acceptance of confederation as the final goal rather than as a transitional measure leading to 'pure' unification; by equating confederation with unification, Kim was implicitly admitting the obstacles to reconciling the systemic differences between North and South.

Kim's proposals came a few months after the second short official dialogue between North and South had broken down. The first series of talks, in 1972–3, was initiated by the South and was facilitated by external change, as dramatized by the rapprochement between the United States and China, the principal allies of the two Koreas. It was a dramatic breakthrough, representing the first official contact for two decades, but elation soon turned to frustration and disillusion. Although talks begun between Red Cross representatives of both sides did lead to the 4 July 1972 North-South joint statement, in which agreement was reached on the three principles for reunification – i.e., independence and exclusion of 'external powers', non-use of force, and national unity 'transcending differences in ideas, ideology and systems' – it soon became clear that both sides interpreted the agreement differently. After President Park introduced his Yushin Constitution and the opposition leader Kim Dae-jung was kidnapped from Japan, the dialogue was called off by the North. The second series, 1979–80, was prompted by internal changes brought about by the assassination of Park, and was initiated by the North, which hoped to make capital out of the resulting political fluidity. Although both sides actually referred to each other by their official names (something that had been studiously avoided previously, even in the 1972 statement), little progress had been made before the seizure of power by General Chun brought the preliminary talks to a halt.

South Korea's reunification strategy has remained less clearly defined than the North's. In the 1960s, President Park pushed for 'economic construction first, reunification later'; even during the 1970s, the South seemed to play a rather defensive role in response to the North's reunification proposals. Chun, however, tried to take some of the initiative away from North Korea and its DCRK proposal. In January, and again in June, 1981, he proposed a summit meeting with President Kim; then, in January 1982, he unveiled his proposals for a Council for Unification to be formed by representatives from both sides to draft a unified constitution which could be submitted to a referendum, and for resident liaison missions to be based in each other's capitals to facilitate twenty pilot cooperative ventures. The North rejected these proposals, refusing to enter a dialogue while US troops were in the South and Chun was in office.

The flow of proposals and counter-proposals and the trading of accusations that the other government was an illegitimate 'puppet' characterized the early 1980s, until the unexpected North Korean offer of relief goods in response to damage caused by heavy flooding in the South, and the South's equally unexpected acceptance of goods in September 1984, paved the way for a number of dialogues to begin between representatives from North and South. These were in four areas: Red Cross, economic, parliamentarian, and sports. A North Korean proposal in June 1986 for talks in a fifth area, military, in which the Americans would be included, has been rejected by the South.

A chronology of these four dialogues can be found in the appendix to this book. The dialogues have been suspended twice, in 1985 from January to April and again in 1986 from January to June (when talks on the Olympics occurred), because of the North Korean refusal to conduct dialogues during the period when the annual joint US-South Korean military exercise, 'Team Spirit', is taking place. The North Koreans have been offered the opportunity, since 1982, to send observers to the exercises (but have declined, as to do so would imply giving legitimacy to the US presence), and the South Koreans have pointed out that talks have taken place in previous years during the exercise period (such as sports talks in April 1984).

These interrupted talks have brought little except for the agreement to allow a small number of separated families to cross over to meet relatives under controlled conditions on the other side of the border in September 1985. The emotional scenes generated by these reunions – the first for ordinary citizens since the Korean War – were used for propaganda purposes by both sides, but they also demonstrated the enduring feelings of Koreans on both sides of the border. They probably also brought home to the people of both Koreas the stark reality of how far they have drifted apart. Each side sent 50 hometown visitors (people separated from their former home town), together with 50 folk-art performers and supporting staff and journalists; of the 100 visitors, only 35 who went to Pyongyang and 30 who went to Seoul were briefly reunited with relatives. The Red Cross talks which led to this brief reunion had begun in earnest in May 1985, with the first full meeting since 1973, and continued after the visits, with South Korea pressing to expand the range and frequency of exchanges, but no further agreement was reached by the time of the second suspension.

There have been five meetings on economic questions since November 1984. The South Koreans have made a number of proposals for promoting trade, including reconnecting the severed Seoul/Shinuiju railway, but the North Koreans have tended to concentrate on trying first to establish common principles and elaborate committee structures. Other differences have appeared: the South is more interested in trade, the North in joint ventures; the South would like to swap its manufactured goods for the North's raw materials, but the North would like exchanges of similar commodities, that is, raw materials for raw materials, etc. The North sees the South's proposals as humiliating; as a result, agreement could not even be reached on the terms of one pilot barter exchange of Southern steel goods for Northern anthracite coal.

Two preparatory meetings to arrange a conference between representatives from both national legislatures have been held since the original North Korean proposal was made in April 1985. However, differences remain between the North's proposal that the eventual conference's first step should be a joint declaration of non-aggression, and the South's contention that such a declaration should be left to top government leaders and that the parliamentarians should concentrate on drafting a unified constitution.

Finally, because of continued North Korean criticism of the IOC's decision to award the 1988 Olympics to Seoul, three meetings have been held between the North Korean and South Korean

55

Olympic Committees in Lausanne, under the auspices of the IOC, since October 1985. The South has rejected the North's position that the Olympics should be jointly hosted (the IOC is already contractually committed to Seoul alone), but has reluctantly shown itself prepared to accept the IOC's compromise proposal to let the North host two sports and the preliminary rounds of the football competition. The North has talked of agreeing 'in principle' but has not clarified its response. The Olympic Games dialogue involves both countries' prestige abroad to a degree that the other dialogues do not; significantly, this was the only one of the dialogues to be active in mid-1986. The South, while reluctant to hand over any of the economic benefits and prestige likely to be derived from hosting the Olympics, is worried that a disgruntled North might violently disrupt the Games. The North is worried that other communist countries might be more reluctant than in the case of the Soviet-led action in 1984 to join any boycott of the Olympics that it might try to institute; on the other hand, opening up its borders to thousands of athletes and spectators, as required by the IOC, raises disturbing prospects for such a closed society.

While these four sets of dialogues have been proceeding in public view, there have also been, since mid-1985, a number of secret diplomatic contacts which could yet lead to an unprecedented summit meeting between Presidents Chun and Kim. Chun did propose a summit meeting in 1981, at a time when the North Koreans were strongly opposed to having any contact with his government. However, after the Red Cross and economic talks began, the North Koreans seemed a little more flexible; in his January 1985 New Year address, President Kim suggested that if those talks made some progress, then a high-level summit could be possible. In a manner that echoed the secret visits of 1972, former North Korean Foreign Minister Ho Dam secretly visited Seoul in September 1985, and, a month later, Chong Se-dong, the Director of the South Korean ANSP, similarly visited Pyongyang. Although no further progress was made, in his New Year address in January 1986, President Chun did venture so far as to say that he 'expected' a summit meeting to take place within the year. Japanese press reports, denied by South Korea, suggest that contacts are continuing behind the scenes. For such a summit to be a success, there would have to be something concrete agreed, but with only the Olympic talks having continued into 1986, any compromise would have to be at a fairly low level.

Despite the fact that both Koreas ought to be interested in a reduction in tension on the peninsula, not least because it would reduce the military burden on their economies, the North-South dialogue, even in its most recent phase since 1984, has had a dismal record. One major obstacle has been the North Korean reluctance to acknowledge that there is a separate government in the South (however illegitimate the North may perceive it to be) functioning and exercising its rule over the South Korean people. In its proposals made public in January 1984 for a 'tripartite conference' involving itself, the United States and the 'South Korean authorities', North Korea went some way to accepting the existence of the Chun government. By allowing the various dialogues to take place and by talking about a possible meeting with the 'person in high authority' in South Korea, the North Korean leaders are going further down this road.

A number of factors may be at play in the North Korean policy. First, the continued drain on the national economy of military expenditure may well have led the economic technocrats to argue that some measure of *modus vivendi* on the peninsula would not only enable more attention to be paid to economic development but might also bring some economic benefits from cooperation or trade with South Korea. Perhaps more importantly, it might well help to develop links with Japan, and ultimately the United States, through the joint-venture law introduced in 1984 and other means, which could bring economic benefits to the North. Second, China, which is concerned about maintaining a peaceful regional environment so as to enable it to pursue its own modernization programmes, has been bringing its influence to bear (see next chapter). Third, by projecting a more reasonable image, North Korea may be able to extend not only economic but also political bridges to Japan and the United States (see next chapter), as well as chip away at South Korea's international support.

For South Korea, a favourable political climate on the peninsula and some kind of political accommodation are useful in attracting further foreign investment and beneficial trade. Faced with competition from other NICs and growing protectionist sentiments in some of its main markets, South Korea sees the communist countries, above all China, as potentially valuable markets. North Korea would be less able to object to South Korea-China trade if North-South economic exchanges were already taking place. President Chun also gains legitimacy in the eyes of both foreign observers and the domestic opposition if the North Koreans, who have been so critical of him as a 'puppet' and 'traitor' in the past, agree to a high-level dialogue. Finally, a significant amount of symbolic capital is at stake in the successful completion of the 1988 Olympics, to which a recalcitrant North Korea could cause disruption. In the immediate future, the South Koreans are prepared to make concessions to ensure the safety of the 1986 Asian Games, which are important not just for showing that South Korea has the facilities and organization to run a major sporting event, but also because disruption could lead to world-wide demands for the 1988 Olympics to be moved to a safer location.

Nevertheless, although both sides are now engaged in this intermittent series of dialogues and both are committed to reunification, the differences in approach are so deep that there is no immediate prospect of reunification under either of the formulas proposed by the two sides. Indeed, the most that can be expected for the foreseeable future is a certain amount of confidence-building, or perhaps tension-reduction, across the border. Although the scenario of the two Germanies seems the most likely eventuality, whereby a certain level of mutual recognition and psychological reconciliation is achieved, the South Koreans still cannot give up the idea that the North favours the Vietnamese solution. The lack of mutual trust affects the pace of reconciliation. So too does the attitude of the four major external powers, who are all, to a lesser or greater degree, reluctant to upset the status quo on the peninsula.

5

THE TWO KOREAS AND THE FOUR MAJOR POWERS

Because of its geographical position, Korea has served both as a buffer and as an invasion route for its more powerful neighbours. The Koreans have been invaded by the Chinese (in the seventh century), the Mongols (in the thirteenth century), the Manchus (in the seventeenth century), and the Japanese (in the sixteenth and twentieth centuries). In the last century alone, three wars have been fought on Korean territory for control and influence over the peninsula – the Sino-Japanese War in 1894–5, the Russo-Japanese War in 1904–5 and, of course, the Korean War, in 1950–3. Korea has been occupied by the Japanese for 35 years, from 1910 to 1945, and by the Russians and the Americans for three years after World War II.

Although the four external powers most directly involved – China, Japan, the Soviet Union and the United States – have expressed support for the peaceful reunification of the Korean peninsula, they are all opposed to the peninsula's control by one dominant power. In the abstract, the two Koreas and the four major powers agree on the need for peace and stability on the peninsula, but there is sharp disagreement on the cause of tension and the means of alleviating it. However, the Korean proverb 'in ten years even the rivers and mountains change' aptly describes the fluid situation in North-east Asia, as compared, for example, with the relatively static geopolitical situation in Europe. For the two Koreas, this fluidity raises prospects of being manipulated by the major powers involved, but it also offers opportunities for diplomatic flexibility. As the two Koreas grow in economic, political and military strength, their freedom of movement will increase.

The US-South Korean alliance

President Chun, like his predecessor, has vigorously sought and received repeated reaffirmations of the US security commitment to South Korea. Although successive South Korean leaders have stressed the reciprocal nature and mutual benefits arising from the bilateral relationship, at least until the 1970s it was a deeply asymmetrical one; South Korea had little perceptible leverage over its principal patron state. US economic and military aid represented as much as 10 per cent of South Korean GNP during the period 1954–70, and not until 1978 was direct US military assistance finally phased out. It was US prodding that made South Korea send troops to fight in the Vietnam War from 1965 to 1973, and, although South Korea's economy benefited significantly from Vietnam-related procurement orders, the costs included Third World criticism of its 'mercenary' role.

In the 1970s, US-South Korean relations were bedevilled by a series of irritations which came to a head during the Carter administration. First, alarmed by the implications of President Richard Nixon's Guam Doctrine, which resulted in the withdrawal of one division of US troops in 1971, the Park government launched a campaign to buy influence with US politicians which, when exposed, became known as the 'Koreagate' scandal. Second, President Carter's emphasis on human rights inevitably brought him into conflict with Park, who was, if anything, instituting more repressive measures internally. Third, President Carter's plan, announced in 1977, for the phased withdrawal of the remaining US ground troops unnerved the South Koreans; although domestic lobbies within the United States secured a reversal of this policy, the Koreans remained suspicious of the depth of the Carter administration's commitment.

The advent of the Reagan administration brought an improvement in relations. President Chun has visited the United States twice, in February 1981 (when he became the first foreign head of state to meet the new US president) and in April 1985; President Reagan visited South Korea in November 1983, when he became the first US president to visit the DMZ. Reagan has assured Chun that there are no plans to withdraw US troops from South Korea, and the security commitment has in fact been upgraded, in the sense that the joint communiqué issued at the end of the Reagan visit in 1983 described the security of South Korea as 'pivotal' to the stability of

North-east Asia and, for the first time, as 'vital' to the security of the United States. Joint security cooperation has increased and the United States has agreed to give the South more advanced military technology, such as the F-16 fighters. Although the Reagan administration has continued to give a high priority to requesting credits for South Korean purchases, which are still increasing in value, US arms sales are affected by Congressional politics and could be restricted by the Gramm-Rudman budget-balancing amendment, which became law in December 1985.

From the US viewpoint, the continuing commitment to keep US forces in South Korea has a number of justifications. First, it deters aggression again by North Korea (for this reason the bulk of the troops are stationed between the DMZ and Seoul). As Henry Kissinger pointed out in his memoirs, the reason for the US commitment to Europe and to South Korea is the same: the removal of the US shield might invite aggression.[11] Significantly, when the US Congress debated the Nunn amendments about US troops in Europe in 1984, no mention was made of reviewing the US commitment to South Korea. Second, it is a credible symbol of US determination to remain an Asian power and to maintain a balance of power in the region. Third, it provides intelligence and surveillance capabilities that the South Koreans still lack. Fourth, it links up with other regional objectives, such as protecting Japan from the threat of any Asian continental power and blocking further Soviet expansionism. For the Reagan administration, South Korea constitutes an outpost in its confrontation with the USSR. In general, the South Koreans understand that this US interest is, thus, primarily geopolitical. Yet the Reagan administration recognizes the uncertainty that would arise from a change in its security commitment in this strategically sensitive area.

Under the Reagan administration the human rights issue has been de-emphasized, at least publicly, but the manhandling of Kim Dae-jung on his return to Seoul Kimpo airport in February 1985 and his subsequent harassment, as well as the police handling of the activities of the university students and the opposition political parties, have led to pressure from concerned US politicians for a higher US governmental profile in pushing for more democratic reform. The administration has been reluctant to be forced into public statements, but has refuted the parallels being drawn between the Philippines and South Korea as being inappropriate. Although it is unlikely that US Ambassador Richard Walker would now repeat his 1982 statement that Korean dissidents were 'spoiled brats who have no public sympathy',[12] and opposition leaders have recently even attended Embassy functions, the US efforts to encourage further democratization have been cautious and low-key.

Tension in the bilateral relationship in recent years, therefore, has arisen less from human rights issues than from trade disputes. US-South Korean trade has arisen from $3 bn in 1973 to $17 bn in 1985, but the balance of trade has moved to South Korea's advantage since 1982, reaching the level of $4 bn in 1985. The United States has continued to be South Korea's leading trade partner, accounting for 28 per cent of trade in 1985 (35 per cent in terms of exports), while South Korea has become the seventh largest trading partner of the United States (having been fifteenth a decade ago). The growing imbalance has prompted US criticism and action, echoing earlier reactions to Japanese trading practices. Quotas, tariffs and anti-dumping duties have been imposed (in 1984 Korean sources estimated that 45 per cent by value of South Korean exports to the United States were under some form of restriction) and a number of products have been removed from eligibility under the GSP scheme. At the same time, considerable pressure has been placed on the Koreans to liberalize their import regulations and adhere to international conventions covering intellectual property rights.

The Koreans have been rather aggrieved by US sentiments and policies, feeling that they have been victimized despite being a loyal ally of the United States. For example, the imposition of a duty of 64 per cent on South Korean photo albums (hardly a significant item in the total bilateral trade) in October 1985 was denounced in front-page headlines in the Korean press. The July 1986 package of measures allowing tobacco imports and agreeing to strengthen patent and copyright protection was also strongly criticized. South Korea's response has been to try to explain that it is not a 'second Japan', to show that measures are being undertaken to open up the economy, to send 'purchasing missions' to the United States, and to try to diversify its trading partners. Whereas in the US-Japanese relationship it has been the United States which has tried to link economic and defence issues (by arguing that some action against Japanese exports might be diverted by greater Japanese defense expenditures), in the US-Korean relationship it is the South Koreans who have tried to link the two issues, by arguing that their economic practices should be given special consideration because of the costs of defending their country against the communist North.

The US-South Korean relationship is less asymmetrical than it was a decade ago, and South Korea is able to demonstrate more independence as its economic and political power grows (one example is the decision in 1980 to purchase French nuclear technology which the Americans had vetoed five years earlier). Nevertheless, the United States continues to play the role of patron state, albeit to a gradually diminishing degree.

The Japan-Korea 'special relationship'

Historically, the United States has been able to exert little leverage over its only two North-east Asian allies to make them improve their own bilateral relationship and so complete a triangle. Public opinion polls in both South Korea and Japan have, with unfailing regularity, depicted the other country unfavourably. In South Korean polls, Japan is invariably placed as the next most hated country after North Korea, while only in recent years has the Japanese Foreign Ministry's annual poll shown those Japanese with friendly feelings towards Korea outnumbering those who are hostile.

A long-standing enmity, the origins of which can be traced back to the early phases of the two countries' histories (Hideyoshi's invasion of Korea in the sixteenth century is but one example), was exacerbated by the brutality and thoroughness this century of the 35 years of Japanese colonial occupation. The legacy of resentment and bitterness among Koreans is still not far below the surface, as shown by the critical reactions in 1982, and again in 1986, to reports that Japanese history textbooks would be altered to sanitize references to the suppression of the Korean independence movement and the forced transportation of Koreans to Japan. Of crucial symbolic importance for the South Koreans, therefore, was the phraseology used by Emperor Hirohito when he received President Chun on a state visit in September 1984. By choosing to describe the 'unfortunate past' as 'regrettable', the Emperor pitched his apology at the level of earlier apologies to American and Chinese leaders, though Prime Minister Nakasone was himself to amplify this into an expression of 'deep regret' for 'great sufferings' inflicted on the Korean people.

The four major powers

Not until 1965, twenty years after the Pacific War, were relations normalized between Japan and South Korea, and Japanese relations with the North have yet to be formalized. Even the 1965 accords represented a marriage of convenience rather than a resolution of emotional conflict. Japan-South Korean relations, however, were relatively cordial from 1965 to 1972, with a heavy influx of Japanese investment and close links between the political and business sectors in both countries. They were strained from 1972 to 1975, when the abduction of Kim Dae-jung from a Tokyo hotel and the assassination of President Park's wife by a Korean brought up in Japan drove a wedge between the two countries, but they returned to comparative cordiality until Park was himself assassinated. Chun endeavoured to relaunch relations on a new basis; he and the new leadership looked at Japan in a more critical light than Park. Speaking in 1981, Chun advocated a 'community of destiny' between Japan and South Korea, but in fact during 1981–2 relations deteriorated over a number of issues: the Korean treatment of Kim Dae-jung, the Korean request for a $6 bn loan from Japan, and the Japanese history textbook revisions. Prime Minister Nakasone's unprecedented visit to Seoul in January 1983 and Chun's to Tokyo in 1984 have done much to improve relations between the two countries, at least at the governmental level, but they have not completely removed emotional tensions between the two peoples.

Economic ties are the key dimension to the South Korean-Japanese relationship. With reluctance, Koreans will admit to the inspirational and material support from Japan for their modernization. Japanese investment had reached $843m in cumulative terms by 1984 (49 per cent of total foreign investment) and aid had reached a total of 718 billion yen. However, as the Koreans complain, the trade balance has been persistently in the Japanese favour, giving bilateral deficits of around $3 bn in both 1984 and 1985. The Koreans claim that this bilateral deficit threatens their ability to service their international debt and, indirectly, contributes to protectionist frictions with other trading partners. Yet, given the reliance of Korean industry on the supply of Japanese capital and intermediate goods, the efforts by the Koreans to increase exports only pull in more imports from Japan.

The second Korean complaint is about the Japanese reluctance to transfer advanced technology to Korea. Japanese businessmen are concerned about the 'boomerang phenomenon', whereby low-cost

64

Korean competition could undercut Japanese dominance in certain products, especially in the high-tech fields. The Japanese government has tried to resist the Korean claim that it can influence technology transfer, which it says is purely a private-sector question. However, by agreeing in 1985 to sign a science and technology agreement, the Japanese went some way to accepting the Korean argument.

The other areas of tension between Japan and South Korea concern internal matters. The Korean community in Japan, a legacy primarily of Japanese forced transportation of Koreans during the colonial period, now numbers around 650,000, but suffers from a range of legal and societal disadvantages. The majority of the Korean community are unaffiliated to the two organizations that claim to represent them: the Mindan (pro-South) and the Chongnyon (pro-North). These are so mutually antagonistic that they are unable to act together in trying to overcome the Japanese discriminatory policies (such as that over finger-printing regulations) and, indeed, seem to function more as subsidiary agents of their respective home governments than merely as organizations representing the interests of the Korean residents in Japan.

Japanese criticism of the South Korean government's actions, particularly over issues such as the Kwangju uprising and the fate of Kim Dae-jung, has aroused resentment not only within the Korean government but even within the opposition movement. Many Koreans who are prepared to risk personal hardship in opposing their government's policies find such Japanese criticism embarrassing, not least because they feel that Japan, given its previous ruthless domination of Korea with little regard for human rights, is hardly in a position to be critical.

Since Nakasone became prime minister, there has been a greater measure of Japanese agreement with South Korea and the United States on security issues, but, whatever North Korea and the Soviet Union may say about a 'tripartite military alliance', there is little prospect of change in the present arrangement, whereby the main axes of cooperation continue to be the separate bilateral alliances with the United States. Most Japanese play down the North Korean threat, even though large-scale military conflict on the peninsula would involve them, at least indirectly; they tend to see it, to use President Chun's own words, as 'a fire across the ocean'. They prefer to concentrate, as Nakasone has repeatedly told the Americans, on the Soviet Union as the main disruptive factor in North-east Asia. Even if constitutional constraints which hinder the use of Japanese forces overseas were to be circumvented, it is inconceivable that emotional legacies would permit joint Japanese action with South Korean forces on Korean soil. Japan's contribution has been, and is likely to remain, confined to the provision of bases to allow American forces to carry out their commitments to defend South Korea.

In public the Japanese have supported South Korean proposals for the reunification of the peninsula, but in practice they have not advanced much beyond vague statements about creating an 'environment for dialogue' on the peninsula. Japan has no diplomatic relations with North Korea, but is by far its largest non-communist trading partner (though bilateral trade totals are paltry by comparison with Japanese-South Korean trade). The Japanese government imposed temporary diplomatic sanctions on North Korea after the Rangoon bombing, but did not halt private-level contacts with North Korean organizations. As part of his general policy of promoting Japan's more active regional role, Nakasone has been willing to explore tentative contacts with the North, based on his assumption that, having first established a sound basis to the Japan-South Korean relationship, he can avoid some of the difficulties his predecessors provoked in the early 1970s. The South Korean government has been watching carefully, and, given the level of Japanese interest and involvement in the South, it is unlikely that Japan will advance too far ahead of South Korean tolerance.

South Korea's Nordpolitik
The South Koreans see Japan as one means of promoting contact with China (and the Japanese are happy to have yet another reason to talk to the Chinese). Since the early 1970s, South Korea has officially maintained a policy of establishing contacts with all countries regardless of ideology, and this policy has been given particular prominence at certain periods, such as in June 1983, when Foreign Minister Lee Bum-suk announced a Nordpolitik (northward policy) to 'normalize relations with the Soviet Union and mainland China'. China has traditionally taken a harder line than the Soviet Union on contacts with South Korea (a South Korean citizen had actually attended an international conference in Moscow

in 1973, something that did not happen in China until 1981), but in the early 1980s it is China that has proved the more responsive to advances from the South. The hijacking of a civilian Chinese airliner to South Korea in May 1983 and the entry of a Chinese torpedo boat into South Korean waters, after a mutiny on board, in February 1985, provided fortuitous opportunities for representatives of both sides to meet. A limited number of contacts, mainly sporting ones, have followed.

Apart from the general desire to gain wider international recognition and legitimacy, the South Korean government has a number of objectives in trying to approach China. Initially, it wanted to encourage China to use its influence to restrain North Korea from engaging in any adventurist military activity. More recently, it has wanted to ensure that this major Asian power would agree to participate in the 1986 Asian and 1988 Olympic Games. The longer-term hope is that China, because of its geographical proximity and size, will become a major trading partner. The economic relationship is already becoming important, with two-way trade – conducted mostly through Hong Kong – rising from $285m in 1983 to over $800m in 1985 according to some estimates; in fact, China's trade with the South may now exceed its trade with the North. Some covert direct trade has begun, a number of senior Korean industrialists have visited China, and Daewoo is starting the first-ever South Korean joint venture in China – to produce televisions in Fujian – this year.

For China, too, these growing official economic links are useful, since South Korea can be an important source of the intermediate goods and technology necessary for modernization, at prices which are competitive with the Japanese. As Chinese resentment against the burgeoning trade deficit with Japan mounts, South Korea seems a perfect foil. China is concerned about any disturbance in its immediate regional environment which might threaten its ability to carry out the 'four modernizations' programme.[13] As such, unofficial contacts with the South might help to maintain peace and stability, though China remains constrained by fears that a critical North Korea will move closer to the Soviet Union.

The Soviets have been more reticent than the Chinese in widening contacts with the South Koreans, and all contacts were broken for nearly a year, anyway, after the destruction of the KAL airliner by a Soviet fighter in August 1983. That action did not alter the South

Korean perception of North Korea as their main threat – it was seen as something symptomatic of communist governments. Although the South does import some Soviet coal unofficially, South Korean indirect trade with the USSR is minimal by comparison with its trade with China. The South Koreans have been concerned and are suspicious about signs of a deepening Soviet-North Korean relationship since Kim visited Moscow in May 1984, as demonstrated by increasingly sophisticated Soviet weapon supplies for the North and the visits of Soviet naval flotillas to North Korean ports. The South wishes to encourage the Soviets (as well as the Chinese) to restrain the North Koreans, but it has fewer opportunities to come into unofficial contact with them (which is one reason why the South Koreans are encouraging West Europeans to talk with the Soviet Union).

Like the Chinese, the Soviets are reluctant to cultivate relations with the South if it means pushing North Korea into the arms of its main communist rival. Convinced as they are that South Korea is firmly embedded within the US-centred alliance system, they see little inducement, economic or otherwise, to make it worthwhile sacrificing the benefits being gained from their connection with the North.

The North Korea/China/Soviet Union triangle

Because it shares borders with both China and the Soviet Union, North Korea has developed special ties with them both; indeed, the lives of the two Kims reflect these ties in a microcosm. The elder Kim fought with the Chinese in Manchuria against the Japanese in the late 1930s, but entered Pyongyang in 1945 with the Soviet troops and wearing a Soviet uniform. His son was born in Khabarovsk but was educated in Jilin. Furthermore, Kim Il-sung has managed to maintain his country's posture of 'equidistance' towards both its allies by siding with one or the other on particular issues but aligning with neither. For example, North Korea opposes the Soviet-backed Vietnamese invasion and occupation of Kampuchea but, after some initial hesitation, supports the Soviet-backed government in Afghanistan. The North's two communist neighbours have continued to be its principal sources of economic, technical and military aid; since the conclusion of mutual defence treaties in 1961, both have been allies in the military sense as well.

After initially relying heavily on Soviet assistance, North Korea was rescued by the Chinese from the UN northward advance during the Korean War, and it continued to grow closer to China as de-Stalinization and peaceful coexistence became operative in the Soviet Union. North Korea then tilted slightly towards the Soviet Union during the 1960s, as relations with China deteriorated during the Cultural Revolution. However, since the end of that xenophobic period in China, Kim has been able, during the 1970s and early 1980s, to maintain workmanlike, if not necessarily warm, relations with both China and the Soviet Union. The Sino-Soviet rift initially posed a problem for North Korea in trying to maintain a semblance of neutrality between the feuding powers, but this was later turned to its advantage by giving it some leverage over both. Judged by the yardstick of mutual visits by top-level leaders, in the second half of the 1970s (after Kim's visit to Beijing in 1975) through to the early 1980s, Sino-Korean relations seemed warmer than Soviet-Korean relations; but since Kim's visit to Moscow in May 1984 (his first since 1961), the picture has gradually reversed. Soviet-Korean relations have improved markedly. Yet, as Sino-Soviet relations themselves slowly improve, North Korea seems again to be trying to balance the level of exchanges with Chinese and Soviet leaders, judging by the visits undertaken to celebrate the anniversaries in July 1986 of North Korea's defence treaties with its two neighbours.

President Kim sees the Soviet Union as a large and potentially threatening neighbour that would like to dominate North Korea as it does Mongolia; he has often declared his opposition to 'domina-tionism' (refusing, however, to endorse the Chinese codeword 'hegemonism') or 'flunkeyism'. Yet, at the same time, the Soviet Union is a crucial ally. Notwithstanding the *juche* philosophy, North Korea has consistently sought economic and military assistance from the USSR. Soviet economic and technical aid has been important for a number of projects directly beneficial to the Soviet Union, such as the construction of a new port at year-round ice-free Najin, which the Soviets use for trans-shipping supplies for Vietnam, and the electrification of the rail-link between Najin and the Soviet railway system. Having been induced by the Soviet Union to sign the Nuclear Non-proliferation Treaty in December 1985, North Korea is now to receive Soviet help in the construction of its first nuclear power plant (the North Korean media have played down the Chernobyl nuclear accident). Although the Soviet Union originally made a significant contribution to modernizing the North Korean armed forces, during the 1970s its direct military aid declined to minimal levels and it showed a marked reluctance to extend the most sophisticated military technology to the Koreans. However, on his trip to Moscow in 1984, Kim was able to secure Soviet agreement to supply Mig-23s, which he needed to compete with the South Korean purchase of F-16s, but at the cost of allowing the Soviet Union to have greater access to Korean facilities, probably at the Wonsan submarine base, and to fly its military aircraft over North Korean airspace, thus extending their southward range from Siberian bases.

In the field of diplomacy, too, Soviet power and influence are valuable to North Korea, particularly in its competition with the South. The Soviet Union has helped to mobilize the support of other socialist and non-aligned Third World countries behind North Korea's claims against the South and against the US military presence there. North Korea joined the Soviet boycott of the Los Angeles Olympic Games and, as shown by the joint communiqué issued after Soviet Foreign Minister Eduard Shevardnadze visited Pyongyang in January 1986 (the first Soviet foreign minister ever to do so), it was, in return, able to secure Soviet support for its campaign to secure a joint Pyongyang/Seoul hosting of the 1988 Olympics (Soviet participation in the Seoul Olympics could imply *de facto* recognition of the South Korean government).

On two political points, however, North Korea has been less successful in soliciting Soviet support. Although the Soviets have agreed with the North Koreans on the dangers of what they see as US attempts to forge a military block with Japan and South Korea, they have been reticent about giving wholehearted endorsement to all North Korean unification policies. When Kim visited Moscow in 1984, President Konstantin Chernenko expressed the desire that the Koreans should be united in 'one peace-loving democratic state', but he did not publicly refer to Kim's proposals for tripartite talks with the Americans and the South Koreans. The North Koreans have also found it difficult to obtain public Soviet support on the succession issue; Kim Jong-il has visited China but has yet to be invited to the Soviet Union.

The Soviet Union has a strategic interest in Korea, not least because of its closeness to Vladivostok, the principal, but not ice-free, base of the Soviet Pacific fleet. Its renewed high-grade military support for North Korea has been used to gain concessions from Kim (such as overflights) which meet wider Soviet strategic requirements in East Asia. As elsewhere on its borders, the Soviet Union wants a friendly government, as responsive as possible to its wishes. However, Kim's North Korea has proved to be an irritating and at times intractable ally. The Soviet Union would like to integrate North Korea more closely into the Soviet bloc, but it has consistently refused to join Comecon, has insisted on maintaining extensive relations with China and, on a number of issues (most notably Vietnam/Kampuchea), has acted contrary to Soviet wishes.

The Soviet Union has been in competition with China for influence in North Korea, but this has not become an issue in the way of Sino-Soviet reconciliation (it does not figure as one of the 'three obstacles' cited by the Chinese). Similarly, Korea is of secondary importance in terms of Soviet relations with the United States. Although the Soviet Union would prefer US troops to be withdrawn from South Korea (and as such has approved of the abortive North Korean initiative in June 1986 for military talks), it probably does not see them as a significant threat to its own territory (though their information-gathering role does affect Soviet air and sea movements in North-east Asia).

The Chinese, in turn, are concerned about signs of growing Soviet influence over North Korea. Unable to supply the kind of advanced military technology that the Soviet Union can, China has nevertheless continued with economic assistance and remains the North's second most important trading partner. It has also been more vocal publicly in supporting the North Korean unification strategies and the tripartite talks proposal. Indeed, it was Chinese Premier Zhao Ziyang who actually transmitted that proposal to President Reagan when they met in Washington in January 1984. The Chinese have resisted subsequent efforts by the Americans both to include China in four-party talks (a suggestion which irritated the North Koreans) and to persuade China to act as host for inter-Korean talks. Finally, the Chinese have been more forthcoming than the Soviets over the succession issue; the younger Kim was invited for a personal visit in June 1983, and Chinese Communist Party Secretary-General Hu Yaobang gave public recognition to the two Kims when he visited Pyongyang in May 1985.

China's most important goal, however, is to maintain peace and stability on the peninsula. Seeing Korea as the 'lips' to its own 'teeth', China intervened in the Korean War for reasons of national interest (its own territory would have been threatened by a UN crossing of the Yalu River) and proletarian internationalism. Now the Chinese concern must be to prevent any recurrence of fighting on the peninsula. The Chinese have often told the Americans and the Japanese, who have sought their help, that they have no control over the North Koreans (Deng once told Carter that he was fed up with people asking him to control the North Koreans), but they have reiterated that the North has no intention of invading the South. Certainly China does not want to jeopardize its chances of achieving its two main priorities – economic modernization and reunification with Taiwan – by risking a military confrontation with the United States over Korea. The Chinese were indirectly critical in public of the North Korean bombing in Rangoon in 1983 (the Chinese press pointedly printed both North Korean and Burmese versions of the events), and they have clearly tried since to reassert their standing as a force for stability in the region.

The Chinese have also been trying to point out to North Korea that if it were to imitate the Chinese method of opening up to the West, it would not only avoid Soviet 'dominationism' but, more important, it would gain Western economic and technological assistance in building up its overburdened economy. When Premier Kang visited China in August 1984, he was deliberately taken to see the new Special Economic Zone in Shenzhen. Similarly, North Korean Vice-President Li Jong-ok, during a visit to Beijing in July 1986, was lectured at length by Deng on the advantages of economic restructuring. However, although the 1984 law on joint ventures clearly owed much to Chinese precedent, North Korea has not gone much further down the Chinese path of opening up to the West.

North Korea, Japan and the United States
North Korea has been vigilant against any signs that its two main allies might move towards acceptance of the 'two Koreas' policy by evolving any formal relations with South Korea. While 'socialist solidarity' must be preserved intact, divisions within the capitalistic world can be exploited, and North Korea has moved a long way towards acceptance of a 'two Koreas' policy in practice in its relations with Japan, and even, to a certain extent, with the United States.

With Japan, North Korea consequently follows a dual policy of criticizing 'reactionary' leaders and the 'revival of Japanese militarism' while, at the same time, trying to promote economic and cultural contacts. The North is determined to undermine Japanese support for the South; however, in its recent public pronouncements it has laid stress on pervasive Japanese military links with the South rather than on economic domination, since it is itself trying to woo Japanese commercial interests. In 1983, the North floated the idea of establishing trade liaison offices in Tokyo and Pyongyang, but South Korean warnings and the North Korean failure to meet the repayments on debts already rescheduled once under a 1979 agreement precluded active Japanese interest in such a move. The North has made use of the pro-North loyalists among the Korean residents, as well as of the two major left-wing opposition parties in Japan, but it has also tried to develop contacts with the ruling Liberal Democratic Party, in a way reminiscent of Chinese approaches in the early 1970s. On the other hand, the Japan Socialist Party, which has traditionally opposed any relations with South Korea, has begun to show more interest in widening contacts there and has overridden North Korean objections in order to develop links with the South Korean opposition party, the NKDP, during 1985–6.

A certain duality also characterizes the North's attitude to the United States. While vilifying the Americans as 'war-thirsty imperialists' propping up successive South Korean 'fascist' regimes, North Korea has on a number of occasions sought to obtain some form of recognition from the United States and to develop some cultural and economic links.

In North Korean eyes, the US domination of South Korea is indisputable and the presence of US troops in the South represents the greatest single obstacle to reunification. Contacts were severed after the Korean War for over two decades, until, in 1974, North Korea for the first time proposed talks with the United States. The United States refused to talk with North Korea unless South Korea was also present, and that has been the US position ever since. The North consistently opposed this alternative (thus a joint US-South Korean proposal for tripartite talks in 1979 was rejected) until the January 1984 proposal conceded that the South Koreans should participate. The precondition of the withdrawal of US forces (obviously unacceptable to both South Korea and the United States) was dropped; instead it was suggested that their removal should become one of the subjects of the talks. The tripartite talks would have had on their agenda a peace treaty to replace the 1953 armistice (to which South Korea was not a party), the adoption of a declaration of non-aggression between the two Koreas, and the preliminaries to a dialogue between the two on reunification. Several points were not made clear, not least whether the two sets of talks (North Korean-US, North-South Korean) were to take place simultaneously or consecutively. President Reagan, aware of the South Koreans' preference for bilateral talks, proposed that there should be either bilateral or quadripartite talks (involving China). The North Korean proposal, though not rescinded, has effectively been shelved while direct North-South discussions have continued since the autumn of 1984; the idea of a non-aggression pact between North and South has been subsumed under the North's proposed agenda for the parliamentary talks.

Both North Korea and the United States point to a series of incidents to justify their distrust of the other: the capture of the US spy ship *Pueblo* in 1968, the downing of a US EC-121 spy plane in 1969, the axe-murder of two US servicemen at Panmunjon in 1976, and the firing of North Korean missiles at SR-71 reconnaissance aircraft in 1981. To the North Koreans, these are heroic acts against predatory foreigners; to the Americans, they are hostile acts by a bizarre regime. President Reagan's inclusion of North Korea in his list of 'terrorist' regimes around the world, in his July 1985 speech, is only the latest expression of that theme. The US government returned in 1985 to the policy initiated in 1983, but revoked after the Rangoon bombing, of granting visas on a case-by-case basis to North Koreans to attend academic conferences, but this should not be taken as presaging a new phase in US policy. South Korean concern is a very real limiting factor. The current US administration, anyway, remains highly suspicious of North Korean intentions, not least because of the signs it has noted of the North's military buildup close to the DMZ.

The more fluid situation on the peninsula in the early 1980s, and the frequency with which leaders of the four major powers have met with each other and with the leaders of their respective Korean allies, have given rise to intermittent reconsideration of the concept of cross-recognition: that is, the United States and Japan recognizing North Korea, and China and the Soviet Union recognizing

South Korea. This was an idea that was briefly given some prominence by US Secretary of State Henry Kissinger in 1975, and it was
revived in 1983 after Nakasone's visits to Seoul and Washington
heralded the birth of a sounder relationship among the non-
communist allies. The North has consistently opposed the idea,
which it sees as meaning the consolidation of the existing division of
the country. However, the growth in Chinese-South Korean and
Japanese-North Korean contacts in 1985–6 suggests that a partial
cross-recognition formula, involving those four countries only and
leaving the Soviet Union and the United States to a later stage, could
become an option.

6

WEST EUROPEAN INTERESTS

President Chun's visit to four West European countries and the EC headquarters in April 1986 was the first such tour ever undertaken by a South Korean president. Less than one month later, Mrs Thatcher became the fifth West European prime minister to visit South Korea in the course of two years. Despite the fact that President Chun's host countries had celebrated, or were about to celebrate, their respective centenaries of the establishment of diplomatic relations with Korea, this flurry of high-level exchanges paradoxically attested to the lack of depth – and even novelty – of their relationship.

Many Europeans know very little about Korea. Their knowledge is limited to media stories of the religious group the Moonies, or to images of the Korean War from the television comedy programme M*A*S*H. Until the middle of the nineteenth century, Europeans had little contact with what they called the 'Hermit Kingdom'; even after the opening up and the establishment of diplomatic relations between Korea and several European countries in the 1880s, the dominant role of Japan hampered contact. Lacking any striking natural or man-made feature to catch the European popular imagination, such as Mt Fuji in Japan or the Great Wall of China, Korea has somehow become indistinguishable from the general European image of East Asia and has failed to gain any clear definition of its own. Geographical remoteness has been compounded by psychological distance. Nor has this situation been changed by the growing presence of Korean businessmen operating in European markets: the Koreans – and their culture – are little known or understood in Europe.

Two non-EC West European countries (Switzerland and Sweden) do have a role to play on the Korean peninsula as part (together with Czechoslovakia and Poland) of the Neutral Nations Supervisory Commission, which monitors the armistice agreement. However, this chapter will tend to concentrate on the EC and its constituent members. It is evident that Western Europe has no vital interests in the Korean peninsula in the sense that, if they were threatened, there would be a direct or immediate effect on the survival of European nations. Nevertheless, there are interests which, if not vital in this sense, are important to the Europeans. For convenience, these can be broadly divided into the economic, politico-strategic, and cultural dimensions.

Economic interests
The comparatively greater growth in South Korea's economy has made it a more attractive economic partner than the North for the Europeans, but at the same time it has come to be regarded as more of an economic threat. During the period 1973–83, South Korea averaged annual real growth rates that were more than three times those of the European countries (7.3 per cent compared with an EC average of 2.1). World Bank figures suggest that its per capita GNP is now only just below that of Portugal, the poorest of the EC countries.

Throughout most of the 1970s, the EC suffered from a trade imbalance with South Korea, with the deficit widening from only $68m in 1973 to $1.5 bn by 1980. This deficit had grown as South Korea's exports to the EC rose more than eightfold while its imports from the EC grew only fivefold. The growth of Korea's imports from the EC has had several hiccups, most severely after 1980, so that not until 1983 did the level recover to that of 1979. As shown in Table 6.1, however, since 1983 the EC's trade deficit has gradually narrowed.

South Korea is not an important trading partner for the EC, representing less than a half per cent of total EC trade, but, for South Korea, trade with the EC is more significant, representing around 9 per cent of its total (in the case of exports, over 12 per cent). Within the EC, West Germany and Britain are South Korea's

Table 6.1 EC trade with South Korea (in $ million)

	1973	1980	1982	1983	1984	1985
Imports	297	2,915	2,467	2,312	2,379	2,637
Exports	229	1,343	1,291	1,463	1,762	2,109

Source: International Monetary Fund, *Direction of Trade Statistics* (Washington, D.C., IMF, various years).

main trading partners; between them in 1985 they accounted for over 60 per cent of the EC's imports from and exports to South Korea.

Provision was made in the Treaty of Rome for cooperation between the EC and developing countries with which it had special relationships; these countries were headed by the former European colonies grouped under the Lomé Convention (first signed in 1975). South Korea has not qualified for a special form of association, since the EC did not see it as being in the same group as India, Pakistan or ASEAN, with which cooperation agreements have been concluded. However, the EC Commission is now belatedly considering a form of cooperation agreement. In 1971, the EC introduced the Generalized System of Preferences (GSP) scheme, a non-reciprocal exemption from customs duties for manufactured and semi-manufactured goods and certain processed agricultural products from developing countries, but in its application the scheme has become 'progressively tougher on the more industrialized Third World countries', of which South Korea is a prime example.[14]

The EC has taken to concluding sectoral arrangements to cover certain products, deemed 'sensitive', which face highly competitive South Korean imports. Nearly 60 per cent of the EC's imports from South Korea are miscellaneous manufactured articles (according to the SITC) such as textiles and footwear. The textile industry was hard hit by recession in Europe from the mid-1970s; imports from the NICs were blamed and the tightening of controls under the Multi-Fibre Arrangement (MFA) particularly affected the Asian NICs. In some product categories the quotas given to South Korea, which has become the EC's third largest textile supplier, were progressively cut back from levels established in previous years. The next five-year agreement reached within the MFA in early August

1986 showed no lessening of the restrictions on the main categories of South Korean textile products.

The EC steel industry has also been under pressure, and so-called voluntary export restraints have been negotiated with South Korea, which agreed to limit exports to the EC to 218,000 tonnes for 1984 and to respect traditional trade patterns as regards the timing of exports, their destination and product mix. In return, the EC agreed to allow Korean steel producers to sell their products at delivered prices (practically the same as those of EC producers) with a certain penetration rebate to ensure competitiveness. More recent EC moves have been against Korean cars and video tape-recorders (VTRs). In January 1983, less than a year after the Hyundai group started selling cars in Britain, the EC, at British instigation, imposed an import duty of 10.5 per cent on all cars after an initial duty-free 10,000 a year have been imported. In July 1985, the EC decided to nearly double the tariff rate on VTR imports with effect from February 1986; although the Japanese are by far the largest export-ers of VTRs to the EC, the South Koreans, who had only begun to export VTRs in the spring of 1985, felt they were being unfairly discriminated against.

In two other sectors, footwear and shipbuilding, the EC has been pushing for Korean restraint in order to prevent further deteriora-tion in the state of European industry. In footwear, South Korea now exports 45 million pairs of shoes per year to the EC and has become the EC's second largest supplier. As a result, the EC has tried to persuade South Korea to make allowances for the 'state of crisis' in the European footwear market. As for shipbuilding, South Korea is now second only to Japan among the world's shipbuilders, and the European shipbuilding nations clearly want to come to some kind of understanding with the Koreans so as to prevent further relative deterioration of the European position. Despite the assertion of the president of Daewoo Shipbuilding in 1983 that South Korea would assume a 'leadership role' in world shipbuilding, overtaking Japan and, in the process, putting many European shipyards out of business, results for 1984 and 1985 suggest that the Koreans are also finding it difficult to cope with the shipping recession.

These actions by the EC against imports from South Korea are strongly reminiscent of action taken against Japanese imports in the second half of the 1970s. Therefore, as if guilty by association, South

Korea is being sucked into EC-Japan trading disputes. For example, the Japanese threat served as the precedent for the EC's imposition of a bilateral arrangement covering steel from South Korea in 1979 despite the fact that the latter was still a minor exporter and its domestic demand in 1978–9 actually took up all its production. A survey made in 1985 by the Korea Traders Association estimated that 30 per cent of its exports to the EC were subject to some form of regulation.

Despite these restrictions, the pattern of imports from South Korea has continued to concern the Europeans. On his visit to Seoul in May 1984, EC President Gaston Thorn stated that although the EC was not opposed to imports from South Korea, it might be forced to act if they grew 'too quickly' and were 'concentrated on a few sectors'. The Koreans look wistfully at Singapore, which benefits from being part of ASEAN, and Taiwan, whose products are less sectorally concentrated; both have managed to export to the EC without the same level of political friction.

The main concerns of the Koreans are the growing number of barriers being imposed by the United States on Korean goods and the growing imbalance in trade with Japan. But they are also keen to prevent protectionist tendencies in the EC, which is demanding more trade protection in those industrial sectors that are losing competitiveness in relation to the developing countries. For all the pledges given to the Koreans by EC representatives about a commitment to free trade, domestic pressures – at least while unemployment remains high – are likely only to increase the tendency to act against certain South Korean products.

Just as the EC-Japan trade disputes have had two points of contention – on the one hand, voluminous but sectorally concentrated Japanese exports and, on the other, a Japanese domestic market that is difficult to penetrate – so the EC has also come to criticize not only South Korea's exporting policies but also its import restrictions on European products. The Europeans have felt, at least until 1980, that, for all the South Korean government's talk of gradually liberalizing import controls, certain important products have remained 'rigorously restricted'. As shown in Chapter 3, more significant dismantling of import barriers has taken place since then. (Despite South Korea's rhetoric, too, about diversifying its trading partners, to the benefit of the EC among others, Japan and the United States continue to dominate: in 1985 they accounted for 20 and 28 per cent respectively of total South Korean foreign trade.) Calculations made by the Korean Institute of Economics and Technology show that, whatever may be the 'real' degree or extent of this import liberalization, the commodity composition of the liberalized import items is not unfairly distributed to the disadvantage of imports from countries other than the United States and Japan.[15] Nevertheless, the Europeans complain, sales are still hindered by high customs duties and emergency 'surge' and 'adjustment' mechanisms that can be imposed to halt any imports that greatly expand.

According to SITC figures, just over 50 per cent of the EC's exports to South Korea are of machinery and transport equipment – the latter primarily marine equipment, which has shown very high growth rates in the early 1980s, accounting for nearly one-quarter of all EC exports to South Korea by 1983. On the other hand, the value of EC exports of machinery (excluding electrical machinery) actually showed a decline in the period 1979–83; yet it is the general machinery and electrical machinery sectors that are due to have the fastest rate of liberalization over the period 1986–8.

The progress made by the Koreans in trade liberalization has not been paralleled by financial liberalization, an area in which the Europeans are particularly interested. Under the conservative step-by-step approach to deregulation of the financial market inaugurated in 1981, completely free capital movements and the abolition of exchange-rate controls will not be realized until 1990 at the earliest. The only access to the equity market for overseas investors is through the medium of six managed funds (totalling only $240m). European investors, who are the main enthusiasts, were encouraged by the announcement in April 1986 of a $30m fund specifically for Europeans, but implementation will now be delayed. The recent relaxation which allows foreigners to hold convertible bonds issued by major Korean companies is, however, a favourable sign.

Until the last few years, the South Korean authorities have been cautious about encouraging direct foreign investment, and, as with trade, the Japanese and the Americans have dominated at the expense of the Europeans. Cumulative totals from 1962 to the end of 1983 show Japan providing 50 per cent, the United States 28 per cent, and the EC 11 per cent. The dominant position built up by the first two countries has not always been welcome to the Koreans.

Indeed, in 1978, it was announced that measures would be adopted particularly to encourage European countries to offset this predominance. The largest EC investor has been the Netherlands (primarily the Philips Electronics company) with more than half the EC total in cumulative value; West Germany and Britain are some way behind. Prior to 1979, there was only one British industrial investment actually in production, but recent years have seen greater British involvement. Like the French, the British have invested mostly in the financial sector and in the iron and steel industries. The Germans, by contrast, have invested mostly in the chemical and pharmaceutical industries.

Although it is true that the basic Korean policy remains one of favouring investment in joint ventures in which the foreign partner owns 50 per cent or less of the business, there are numerous exceptions to that rule, especially in projects with a higher technology component. The Europeans have had some disappointing experiences, such as British Petroleum's failed application to start a joint venture with Samsung to bottle liquefied petroleum gas. However, the new regulations introduced in July 1984 to simplify administrative procedures, whereby the previous 'positive' list was replaced by a 'negative' list of only those prohibited and restricted products which require the express permission of the relevant ministries, are seen as encouraging. The Europeans have been concerned about the lack of legal protection for intellectual property rights, but have generally left the Americans to take the lead in pressing for Korean adherence to the appropriate international conventions in this field.

South Korean investment in Western Europe is still extremely limited ($10.7m over the 1968–85 period), with the only current major investments being Jindo in Britain and Samsung in West Germany and Portugal. The Irish Republic, however, is likely to receive some investment by Korean electronics companies during 1986, and further investment inside the EC can be expected if the Koreans, like the Japanese, come to see it as a means of circumventing more stringent EC import restrictions.

The EC and South Korea are likely to find themselves increasingly in competition in third markets. Although joint ventures and cooperation in third-market projects do occur – and it has been estimated that as much as two-thirds of the construction materials used overseas by South Korean companies originate in Europe – the

Europeans tend to see the Koreans primarily in a competitive light. It has been suggested that the NICs and Europe should effectively gang up against the main competition, Japan, since neither can face the competition alone; but the increasing willingness in recent years of the Europeans to look for ways to cooperate with the Japanese, both in Europe and in developing countries, makes any such EC-South Korean axis against Japan inconceivable. Joint research and development, however, may be one way for European and Korean companies to collaborate. Until this year, the transfer of technology has been a one-way process from Europe to Korea, but the technology gap is narrowing, particularly in such fields as microchips and robotics. In February 1986, a West German company signed a contract for the transfer of production technology for a new copper alloy for semi-conductor lead-frames developed by Korean researchers, the first such example of the export of Korean technology. The bilateral science and technology agreements which South Korea signed with Britain, France and Germany in 1985–6 are likely to lead to greater cooperation in these areas.

Although direct (and even portfolio) investment has increased considerably during the 1980s, the major, and indeed continuing, source of foreign capital for Korean economic development for the past two decades or so has been loans. The European banks are heavily involved in Korea's massive external debt. Over the 1959–83 period, the EC countries provided $5.2 bn, representing 20 per cent of Korea's total loans (for private loans the percentage rises to 29), and Britain is the third largest creditor after Japan and the United States. Because of its high per capita GNP, South Korea has not qualified for EC aid since 1979, but bilaterally the EC member countries have given about $20m annually in recent years. West Germany has been by far the largest donor and, according to OECD statistics, it provided $18.7m out of an EC total of $27m in 1984.

The EC's economic interaction with North Korea has been limited and difficult by comparison with EC-South Korean relations. During the 1980s, trade has averaged $100m per year for EC exports to, and $150m for EC imports from, North Korea. Even at that low level, trade is not without its problems; in February 1986, Britain had to apply to the EC for restraints on imports of North Korean steel. Even the Scandinavian countries, which have recognized the North, have built up little significant trade under the North's past trading policies. Precise details of North Korean trade are elusive, but the EC is certainly well behind the North's three major trading partners, the Soviet Union, China, and Japan. Memories of North Korea's overdue repayments on credits taken up during 1972–5 still inhibit commercial intercourse. The Sixth KWP Congress in October 1980 underlined the need to diversify foreign trade partners, but Japan has remained the centre of attraction among non-communist trading partners. The announcement in September 1984 of a new law encouraging joint ventures with firms from capitalist countries, inspired by China's efforts to use the West for its own modernization programmes, has not been greeted with great enthusiasm within the EC. So far only the French are involved in a joint venture, to build a hotel in Pyongyang, construction of which was due to begin in March 1985 but has been delayed because of arguments over a suitable site.

The South Koreans are very worried that advanced technology with military applications might be made available to the North, and the revelation in February 1985 that 87 *Hughes* helicopters had reached North Korea via a West German firm only reinforced South Korean efforts to dissuade the West Europeans from any closer economic links with the North. However, until the North Koreans indicate a willingness to talk realistically about their debts, it is doubtful that the Europeans will wish to get involved in any large-scale trading or investment.

Political and strategic interests

Political and strategic interests cannot easily be separated from economic interests, not least because economic development, to which trade and investment from Europe and elsewhere contribute, is commonly accepted as being linked with political stability. Europeans should be concerned not only about stability within the two Koreas but also about the security of the region as a whole. Over the past decade, East Asia has become more and more important geostrategically for the two superpowers, each of which has a military alliance with one of the protagonists on the Korean peninsula. Any escalation of tension which might lead to a second Korean War would have immediate global implications.

South Korea established diplomatic relations with the EC in 1965 and maintains contact through its diplomatic representatives in Brussels. The EC does not yet have a delegation in Seoul – the nearest one is Tokyo – despite South Korean requests, although the Commission does aim to establish one by the end of the decade. Mrs Thatcher, on her visit to Seoul in May 1986, in fact expressed her support for the idea of opening an EC delegation in Seoul. After a Euro-Korean symposium on trade and investment which was held in Brussels in September 1981 on the initiative of the Koreans, it was decided to hold annual consultations at ministerial level, alternating between Seoul and Brussels. These have been held in March 1983, July 1984 and, most recently, in November 1985, when Willy de Clerq, EC Commissioner for External Relations, led a delegation to Seoul.

None of the EC countries has any formally structured alliance arrangements with South Korea. Troops from several European countries fought in the UN forces during the Korean War, but only Britain still contributes, through the Commonwealth Liaison Mission, a token force of about 30 soldiers to the honour guard of the United Nations Command. One senior British officer also participates in the UN representation at the Military Armistice Commission. In October 1985, for the first time for twenty years, the French assigned a liaison officer to the UN Command. This limited European involvement is, nevertheless, valued by South Korea, and by the United States, for the way it symbolizes the continuation of international support. The European powers, however, look to the United States to protect their interests against any direct threat from North Korea, and the Americans claim that their contribution to South Korean security also contributes to West European security, in the sense that an insecure South Korea could divert US attention away from Europe.   Only Denmark and Portugal of the EC countries have diplomatic relations with North Korea, but there is little evidence to suggest that North Korea has been able to use them as a window to the EC. There are North Korean representatives at Unesco and in a trade office in Paris, and at the FAO in Rome; North Korea's admittance to the International Maritime Organization in April 1986 will allow it to send representatives to the IMO's London headquarters. Britain, despite its usual pragmatic policy of recognizing an established government regardless of its political hue, has not moved towards official relations with North Korea, and, indeed, except for France, little serious consideration has been given by the majority of the EC countries to periodic feelers put out by North Korea.

François Mitterrand led a French Socialist Party delegation to North Korea in February 1981, but since becoming president he has been rather cautious in moving towards recognizing the North. In the summer of 1982, it did seem as if the French Foreign Ministry was giving the question serious consideration, but a combination of South Korean diplomatic and commercial pressure (the South feared that Greece and possibly Italy might follow a French precedent) and domestic political undercurrents forestalled action. The Rangoon bombing seemed to confirm that, as Laurent Fabius, then Minister of Industry and Research, said during a visit to Seoul in December 1983, the question of recognizing North Korea 'n'est pas d'actualité'. Nevertheless, shortly after Fabius became prime minister, the French government appeared to make a gesture towards North Korea by authorizing, to South Korean annoyance, a change of description of North Korea's Paris 'trade mission' to 'general delegation'. South Korea responded by postponing a planned French ministerial visit and threatening commercial retaliation. However, when Fabius himself visited Seoul in April 1985, he adopted such a conciliatory line that he even pledged not to recognize North Korea without the consent of the South Korean government.

The French shifts in policy, which may be more apparent than real, have created uncertainties and suspicions in the minds of the South Koreans. In their view, any move towards West European recognition of North Korea must be predicated on two developments: reciprocity, that is, East European recognition of South Korea; and sufficient progress in the North-South dialogue. The South Koreans have seen Western Europe as a possible source of help in their efforts to widen contacts with communist and Third World countries. On his return from a trip to Seoul in 1982, Claude Cheysson, the French Foreign Minister, indicated that he had previously discussed the recognition of South Korea several times with officials from certain East European countries, and in April 1984, Sir Geoffrey Howe, the British Foreign Secretary, offered to encourage certain countries with which Britain has strong links to recognize South Korea.

European political leaders have been generally supportive in public of South Korean proposals for reunification and of what Sir Geoffrey Howe has called South Korea's 'attempts to establish a rational dialogue with the North'. However, in practice the EC countries have tended to leave the attempts to promote some kind of dialogue between the two Koreas to the four powers most directly concerned (the United States, Japan, China and the Soviet Union). They nevertheless have an interest in political stability on the peninsula, and in less tension not only between but also within the two countries. There has yet to be a peaceful transfer of power in South Korea, and disturbances such as those during 1979–80 carry costs which are bound to concern the Europeans.

European governments have been less vocal about the South Korean human rights record than the Carter administration or certain Japanese governments. Even so, the trial and sentencing to death of the leading opposition figure, Kim Dae-jung, in the autumn of 1980 did produce some diplomatic pressure from Europe. The French Foreign Minister, Jean François-Poncet, even postponed a scheduled visit to Seoul – he went in April 1981, after Kim's death sentence had been commuted. All the European governments which Chun visited in April 1986 referred to the need for further democratization, and the West Germans, who after all have experience of an open and flexible democratic system in a divided country, were the most outspoken.

Cultural relations
The culture gap between Europe and South Korea remains a significant one, despite the efforts of several European countries to link exhibitions and visits by artists to the diplomatic centenary celebrations which have been taking place over the past few years. British examples are the visit of the Royal Ballet to Korea and of the art exhibition 'Treasures from Korea' to London. However, compared with the level of Euro-Japanese or Euro-Chinese exchanges, much remains to be done if there is to be greater mutual understanding between the two cultures.

In the educational field, the American influence over the South Koreans has been very strong. Recent estimates suggest that there are 12,000 South Korean students in the United States but only 2,000 in Europe. In the academic year 1984–5, there were only 147 Korean students on British university courses. Eighty per cent of the Korean university lecturers with doctorates obtained them in the United States. The postwar 'hangul generation' in South Korea (those born and educated after 1945) may be more distant from the

Japanese than their parents but they are no closer to the Europeans than their elders. English is required throughout much of the school career, but most Koreans have little chance to practise other European languages. Yet the 1988 Olympic Games are likely to bring an influx of over 300,000 tourists and, as complaints made at the time of the 1985 IMF meeting in Seoul suggest, there are still not sufficient Koreans fluent in foreign languages to cope with the expected demands. The Europeans have been pressing for better conditions for foreign-language teaching in South Korea; in particular the British Council has been trying to maintain its educative role.

Inside South Korea, there are a few centres of European studies, such as those at Yonsei and Seoul National Universities, which allow staff and students to escape from the narrow confines of country specialization and achieve a more balanced perspective on contemporary Europe. Korean studies in Europe are confined to a handful of universities, and unfortunately few undergraduate courses in other universities contain more than a passing reference to Korea. Links are being developed between European and Korean universities, though these tend to be on a departmental rather than on a broader institutional level. Scientific link-ups have been prominent; in the spring of 1986, the Koreans announced plans to construct a science hall for Korean scientists in West Germany and to place up to 900 scientists in British universities till the year 2000 for post-doctoral research.

There has been much unevenness in the coverage of European and Korean developments by the media of the two societies. European journalists find it difficult to extract information from South Korean authorities, partly because such coverage as exists is almost entirely undertaken by Tokyo-based correspondents who visit briefly and have little, if any, knowledge of the Korean language, and who often see events through the prism of Japan. Until recently, the Korean media has tended to concentrate on outdated clichés of European life-styles or on the socio-economic ills of 'decaying' countries; this is symptomatic of an unfamiliarity with the changing European scene.

There is a need, then, for both the Europeans and the Koreans to reduce the psychological and cultural distance between them. Geographical distance is not the only barrier; any trading or economic exchange has cultural elements, and European entrepreneurs are unlikely to perceive opportunities – or profit from them – in an environment such as Korea without a great deal of effort, greater cultural flexibility and a willingness to adjust trading and production methods. A report submitted to the University Grants Committee in Britain in early 1986 identified 'a gradual awakening on the part of British firms to the disadvantages of inadequate familiarity with the customs, languages and culture' of Asia. The Korean language itself was identified as one of regional significance, whose commercial and political importance was 'clearly growing'. The South Koreans have set 1988 as the date for their leap from the Third to the First World; that means that the Europeans can no longer postpone trying to learn and understand more about this ambitious country and its more fractious northern neighbour.

7
CONCLUSION

Towards stability

The Korean peninsula remains an unpredictable area of tension. In the three decades or so since the end of the Korean War, the Koreans north and south of the artificial border have rebuilt their economies and reinforced their nationalistic pride. Their pervasive sense of encirclement by unfriendly neighbours has only intensified their stubborn inner self-sufficiency. The two Koreas have indeed grown, but only further apart; systemic, ideological and value differences have become firmly fixed.

Although both presidents, Kim and Chun, talk about reunification within their lifetime, that possibility remains remote. South Korea does not accept the division of the peninsula as final but has come to recognize and accept its current reality. North Korea not only does not accept the division but also tries to avoid recognizing its existence. Reunification is an emotional and cherished issue for Koreans both sides of the artificial border – and the governments of both sides have on occasion made use of it for their own political purposes. However, the halting dialogue since 1984, including, ironically, the exchange of family visits in 1985, has exposed the reality of how far apart the two still are. With the majority of the population in both South and North consisting of those born since the division occurred, the potency of the issue as one of immediate practical politics is declining, at least in the South.

If, as has been argued in Chapters 4 and 5, in the medium term the confirmation of the existing territorial status quo is more likely than peaceful reunification, will the relationship between the two become more stable and less tense, in the manner of the two Germanies? Given the continued efforts by both sides to obtain increasingly sophisticated weaponry, the immediate prospects for arms control look poor. The first phase would have to be some kind of confidence-building or (perhaps more accurately) tension-reducing measures. For example, the direction of the annual US-South Korean joint military exercise 'Team Spirit' has been changed from north-south to east-west; a reduction in scale might be the next step. The North is already lagging behind the South in economic terms and, within the next few years, despite Soviet assistance, is likely to be so in military terms as well. Although the South will continue to remain suspicious of the North's words and actions, it can be argued that, given the practical constraints, the option of a full-scale invasion must remain more theoretical than real for North Korea; however, that does not rule out the use of military means that fall short of outright incursion.

In the North, the conjunction of the succession from father to son with the need to revamp an economy which is falling behind in the race for supremacy with the South will produce ideological strains. The result, however, could be a more technologically oriented and less isolated society, if the economic technocrats have their way and the oppressive personality cult is scaled down under the younger Kim. Dialogue with the South would then be not just a tactical manoeuvre but a real policy change.

In the South, where society is becoming increasingly pluralistic and sophisticated, the rising demands for a share of the political cake to match the level of economic development complicate the succession issue. The government and the parliamentary opposition have begun to tread carefully in the South's often volatile political arena; yet social justice and pluralism may not come as rapidly as the opposition hopes. Chun has become more politically astute during his years in power, but he is faced with a difficult problem in managing the succession in a way that could satisfy both the radical opposition and those military leaders still on active service. For the foreseeable future the army, and its retired officers, are certain to remain a powerful force in South Korean politics.

The overthrow of President Ferdinand Marcos in the Philippines has led many observers to anticipate parallel developments in South Korea. While both Marcos and Chun have had little time for Western notions of democracy, there are significant differences.

Chun has not adopted the ostentatious life-style of Marcos; neither is corruption so prevalent. Moreover, Chun presides over a healthy economy (by contrast with recent negative growth in the Philippines) with a more equitable distribution of the fruits of economic success. Marcos faced debilitating *internal* communist and Muslim insurgencies; the South Korean government is faced by a widely distrusted *external* communist power. The South Korean army is a much more cohesive and effective force than the Filipino military and has shown no signs of lessening its backing for Chun. Furthermore, Marcos was never able to control the media and use military and police force to overcome the opposition in the way that Chun has managed to do, at least until recently.

In both Koreas, therefore, there is the likelihood of some instability in the immediate future, but with the promise of greater stability both internally and in the inter-Korean relationship in the not too distant future.

A wider international role

The relationships between the two Koreas and the four major interested powers (China, Japan, the Soviet Union and the United States) are likely, as shown in Chapter 5, to remain complex and at times contradictory. All four major powers have officially expressed abhorrence at the idea of a new war in Korea and have approved the inter-Korean dialogue (even if they have discreetly stayed away from direct involvement). They are unlikely to move far from this rather negative or passive involvement in the peninsula's affairs. Given that these powers generally prefer a divided Korea so long as it is peaceful, the pressures for cross-recognition, or partial cross-recognition, are likely to increase.

Nevertheless, the Korean peninsula will remain one of the two areas in East Asia (the other being Indo-China) where local stability and security is closely intertwined with the regional, and global, interests of the Soviet Union and the United States, and, to a lesser extent, of China and Japan.

North Korea faces a particularly complicated adjustment to its foreign policy if it continues down the path of gradually opening up to the outside world. It has already shown signs of extending economic links with the Soviet Union, while at the same time trying to whet the Japanese commercial appetite. In the longer term, this might well require a decision between greater integration into the Soviet/Comecon bloc or closer links with Japan and the rest of the capitalist world, including even the United States.

South Korea already plays an important role in the international economy, having become a leader of the NICs. Its trading activities have given it strong links with the OECD countries and the Middle Eastern oil producers. The momentum for export-led growth will continue, but trade frictions are likely to increase if the product and market concentration of South Korea's exports persist in the face of slower growth rates for world trade and increasing protectionism in its major markets in the coming years. As South Korea appears to be increasingly strong in the world market, thereby seemingly confirming apprehensions of it as a 'second Japan', the developed countries may be reluctant to absorb its past levels of exports. South Korea will then have to take a more active role in international economic organizations, above all the GATT (particularly when the new round begins). Certain officials within the Korean government see their country as making a virtue out of necessity by playing a bridging role between developed and developing countries, perhaps by offering concessions on the liberalization of services in return for a standstill on protectionism.

In keeping with their aspirations for greater international status, the South Koreans are not averse to thinking about longer-term economic development. However, the degree to which South Korea's growth potential is determined by demand in other countries must cast some doubts on the projections issued by the Korea Development Institute for the year 2000. At around 6 per cent growth per annum, per capita GNP would be just over $5,000 (in 1984 prices) by the year 2000 (the level of Ireland now); in terms of both productive capacity and market size, the Korean economy would be comparable to India or Australia. Although South Korea will probably not achieve its objective of gaining membership of the OECD by its target year of 1988, it will nevertheless be well on the way by then to its transition from the Third to the First World.

West European interests

For the West Europeans, the economic dimension is likely to continue as the main feature of their relationship with South (and even North) Korea. Although the political and cultural aspects are growing in importance, they will remain secondary. Certain propositions arise from the analysis in the earlier chapters.

(1)   The South Koreans are currently involved in an intense, and possibly even slightly counter-productive, campaign to persuade Western countries that their country is not a 'second Japan'. While the method of South Korean exporting seems reminiscent in particular of Japanese approaches, the Europeans should avoid over-simplified comparisons with Japan (in terms of external debt and defence expenditure, at least, there are differences). Although it was not the European intention, the Koreans have occasionally gained the impression, for example during the debate over imposing tariffs on VTR imports in 1985, that there is a measure of collusion between the Europeans and the Japanese in victimizing the newer South Korean exporters. Freer consultation with the Koreans at an earlier stage could have helped to lessen such fears. For Europeans, reciprocity in trade matters is important. It should be made clear to the South Koreans that one of the best counters to protectionism against their products in the European market is for them to push ahead with their own liberalization of imports.

(2)   South Korean economic planners admit to the lop-sided nature of their foreign trade, which is dominated by Japan and the United States. Following Chun's European tour, the Korean government and business representatives have talked about encouraging European imports. In the area of capital goods, however, where the competition is most fierce and where established business connections – especially with Japan – are strongest, it is difficult for Europe to compete. As Korea increasingly imports skill-intensive and high-technology goods, it is to these sectors that Europe should devote sales efforts. One British example is the £30m order for naval command-and-control equipment recently secured by Marconi-Ferranti. The Europeans should take advantage of the South Korean government's current enthusiasm for joint ventures and inward investment from Europe. The planned October 1986 official-businessmen mission to Western Europe has already designated certain target industries (from Britain, farm machinery, car parts and boilers). One characteristic of European as compared with Japanese and US investment in South Korea is the relatively large sums invested per project; the Europeans should consider also

investing with the wide network of small and medium-sized firms which are a major feature of the Korean economy. Picking such a suitable partner will require the assistance of a good trade representation in Korea.

(3)   European financial institutions are likely to find an increasing number of opportunities in trade financing and leasing, and, to a lesser extent, in project financing. With the phasing-out of discriminatory restrictions on foreign banks since 1984, in the longer term greater involvement in direct and portfolio investment may prove to be more worthwhile than the loan capital markets. Although the prospects for foreign-based investors could be affected unfavourably if the Korean authorities have to resort to currency depreciation to achieve their economic targets, the Europeans should be prepared to raise their exposure and press for the planned liberalization of what should become an important market for portfolio investment.

(4)   The EC has already established delegations in Bangkok and Jakarta in the developing East Asian countries; its attempt to run a Korean representation from the Tokyo office is not well received by Koreans. The establishment of an EC delegation in Seoul would have both symbolic value and practical significance in the development of European contacts.

(5)   It is in the European interest to encourage the United States to maintain its political and military support for South Korea for the moment, primarily to deter North Korea from attacking the South, but also, possibly, to restrain the South from taking any precipitate action against the North (President Reagan's call for restraint was crucial in the immediate aftermath of the 1983 Rangoon bombing).

(6)   The Europeans should resist the idea that the French commitment in 1985 not to recognize North Korea without South Korean approval gives the South Korean government an effective veto over European policy towards the North. The Europeans do not have the links with North Korea that the Japanese have, but they might draw on the example of Japan's current policy. While reassuring the South about their dislike for the North Korean system, and having established a firm basis to the South Korean-West European relationship, they should consider developing non-political contacts with North Korea, because of the moderating influence on the latter that greater exposure to outside values, in the

broadest sense, may have. North Korean scholars could be allowed easier access to academic conferences held in Europe, and commercial contacts should be encouraged if the economic benefits seem to justify them.

(7) Particularly now, as relations between Eastern and Western Europe seem to be improving, there are opportunities for the West Europeans to encourage their Eastern neighbours not only to participate in the 1988 Seoul Olympics but also to develop greater indirect, and direct, contact with South Korea. The Chinese and the South Koreans have established a number of informal channels of communication (most notably in Hong Kong), but the Europeans could help to facilitate contacts in third countries between South Korea and the Soviet Union. The next stage, along the lines of the Israelis opening a visa section in the Dutch Embassy in Warsaw in late 1985, could be some kind of token diplomatic representation.

(8) Although the Europeans do not have the political and economic leverage of either the United States or Japan, they are less handicapped by emotion and should be able to encourage the Chun administration to move further towards a democratic system which would be better able to cope with external and internal pressures. The continual references to democratization by his European hosts may have helped to persuade Chun to be more flexible on his return home.

(9) As the Koreans consider sending more graduate, and particularly postgraduate, students to countries other than Japan or the United States for overseas study, European universities, and companies, should be especially encouraging. Industrial benefits could come from linking high-level training in companies with education at a university or polytechnic, though European companies need to be persuaded that the Koreans are not trying to 'get technology on the cheap'.

(10) As interest in South Korea grows with the approach of 1988, there will need to be more committed coverage by the European media. At the same time, the Europeans should do more to promote knowledge about Europe. In the British case, one way would be for the BBC World Service to broadcast in the Korean language – which, in theory, could be received by a combined population of 60 million people – since, at the moment, Korean is the only major East Asian language in which the BBC does not broadcast. British television has run a number of detailed series on life in Japan and

China, and West German television is now filming a major series on Korea; the time has come for similar British treatment.

Above all, it is in Europe's interest to register its commitment to closer links with South Korea, particularly at a time when the latter is looking to diversify its commercial relationships. The commitment made for the first time at the 1985 Bonn summit was one way of doing this;[16] so too is the exchange of senior politicians. In many East Asian countries – as the Europeans have found out to their cost with the ASEAN group – high-level visits are not simply a matter of diplomatic protocol; they are an indication of interest. The Europeans' discussions with South Korea are likely, in due course, to follow the pattern of their dialogues with other Asian partners, such as Japan and ASEAN, in tending to move away from the preoccupation with bilateral economic issues to cover broader political and strategic questions. The opportunities are there to avoid the somewhat sterile route that EC-Japanese relations took in the second half of the 1970s.

APPENDIX: NORTH-SOUTH DIALOGUES SINCE 1984

1984

January	North Korea proposes 'tripartite talks' (NK/SK/US) leading to non-aggression declaration and then talks on reunification
April–May	Three meetings about a joint Korean team for the Los Angeles Olympics
20 August	President Chun proposes trade and economic cooperation with North Korea
September	North Korean relief goods sent to South Korean flood victims
15 November	First trade and economic cooperation meeting
20 November	Preparatory working-level Red Cross meeting

1985

9 January	Further Red Cross and economic meetings postponed by NK because of SK/US 'Team Spirit' exercise
February	IOC proposes NK/SK talks about 1988 Olympics
9 April	North Korea proposes parliamentarians meeting
17 May	Second trade and economic cooperation meeting
27–30 May	Eighth full Red Cross meeting agrees on hometown visit of families (the seventh meeting had been held in July 1973, the last of a series beginning in August 1972)

20 June	Third trade and economic cooperation meeting
23 July	First preliminary joint parliamentary meeting
27–28 August	Ninth full Red Cross meeting
18 September	Fourth trade and economic cooperation meeting
20–23 September	50 hometown visitors and 50 folk-art performers visit each other's country
25 September	Second preliminary joint parliamentary meeting
8–9 October	First IOC-hosted NK/SK talks in Lausanne
20 November	Fifth trade and economic cooperation meeting
3–4 December	Tenth full Red Cross meeting

1986

8–9 January	Second IOC-hosted talks
20 January	Further Red Cross and economic meetings postponed by NK because of SK/US 'Team Spirit' exercise
10–11 June	Third IOC-hosted talks
17 June	North Korea proposes NK/SK/US military talks

NOTES

1. Since the American writer William Griffis first used the phrase 'Irish of the Orient' in a book published in 1882 (*Corea: The Hermit Nation*), the parallels in history and national character between the Irish and the Koreans have been often noted. Certainly, some Koreans see themselves, and the Irish, as an ebullient yet poetic and moody people to which history has not been kind. During the Japanese rule of Korea, many Koreans compared their plight to that of the Irish subjugated by the British and sang patriotic songs to Irish rebel tunes with similar themes (*Korea Herald*, 16 March 1986).
2. The political structure is examined in detail in the contributions by Chin-wee Chung and Dae-sook Suh in Robert Scalapino and Jun-yop Kim (eds), *North Korea Today* (Berkeley, Institute of East Asian Studies, 1983).
3. The ideological contributions of the two Kims are analysed in James Cotton, 'North Korean Marxism and the issue of political succession' (forthcoming in *China Quarterly*, 1987).
4. BBC, *Summary of World Broadcasts*, 26 June 1986, FE8295.
5. See the work of Tony Michell, as summarized in 'Domestic Bliss? Lessons from Korea's economic development 1960–1982', *Euro-Asia Business Review*, Vol. 2, No. 2, pp. 22–7.
6. *Korea Herald*, 27 June 1986.
7. See several articles since 1982 in the Soviet quarterly *Far Eastern Affairs*, as well as M.E. Trigubenko, *Koreiskaya Narodno-demokraticheskaya Respublika* (Moscow, Akademiya Nauka, 1985).
8. BBC, *Summary of World Broadcasts*, 5 January 1980, FE6311.
9. Survey quoted in Sang-woo Rhee, 'The Roots of South Korean Anxiety about National Security', in Charles Morrison (ed.), *Threats to Security in East Asia-Pacific* (Lexington, Mass., Lexington Books, 1983), p. 67.
10. BBC, *Summary of World Broadcasts*, 13 July 1985, FE8002.

11. Henry Kissinger, *Years of Upheaval* (Boston, Little Brown, 1982), p. 308.
12. *Far Eastern Economic Review*, 14 May 1982.
13. For a fuller discussion of China's overall foreign policy objectives, see David Goodman, Martin Lockett and Gerald Segal, *The China Challenge*, Chatham House Paper No. 32 (London, Routledge and Kegan Paul for the RIIA, 1986).
14. Louis Turner, 'Western Europe and the NICs', in Louis Turner and Neil McMullen, *The Newly Industrializing Countries: Trade and Adjustment* (London, George Allen & Unwin for the RIIA, 1982), p. 137.
15. Chung-soo Kim, 'Development and Liberalization of the Korean Economy from the Perspective of Korea-Europe Economic Relations' (Seoul, Korean Institute of Economics and Technology, April 1985, unpublished paper).
16. The 'political declaration' referred to the summit members' hope for the creation of a 'political environment' which would allow the division of the Korean peninsula to be overcome 'in freedom'.

Related titles

The China Challenge: Adjustment and Reform
David S.G. Goodman, Martin Lockett and Gerald Segal

The decade since Mao's death in 1976 has been a period of dramatic changes in China. This paper examines the forces behind the changes, the further reforms currently proposed, the prospects of those reforms being carried out, and the consequences for China and its partners of their successful implementation. The authors consider in turn the political, economic and international dimensions of developments in China, as well as their interaction. They then assess the prospects for continuing reform, for stability or instability in policies, and the implications for other countries of China's likely development over the next few years.

David S.G. Goodman is Director of the East Asia Centre and Reader in Chinese Politics at the University of Newcastle upon Tyne. Martin Lockett is a Research Fellow of Templeton College (The Oxford Centre for Management Studies), specializing in the Chinese economy, and in management and foreign investment in China. Gerald Segal is a lecturer in the Department of Politics, University of Bristol.

Industrial Collaboration with Japan
Louis Turner

This study looks at the experiences of European and American companies that have collaborated with their Japanese competitors in the fields of computers, consumer electronics, automobiles and aero-engines, by forming joint ventures, designing products together and pursuing complementary marketing strategies. It examines why these companies have chosen to collaborate rather than compete; whether the Japanese companies have proved to be reliable partners; whether the non-Japanese have been left behind; and what the future of such collaboration may be. The paper concludes by pointing to a growing interest among non-Japanese companies in investing and collaborating within Japan itself.

This is a particularly timely piece of work, since some of the key collaborations (for example, between Honda and the Austin-Rover Group) have started to produce very positive and promising results. It explores different national and corporate approaches to collaboration, and the different strategies and assumptions that lie behind them.

Routledge & Kegan Paul